The Iron Cow of Zen

The
Iron Cow
of Zen

ALBERT LOW

Charles E. Tuttle Company
Rutland, Vermont & Tokyo, Japan

*Published by the Charles E. Tuttle Company, Inc.
of Rutland, Vermont & Tokyo, Japan
with editorial offices at
2-6 Suido 1-chome, Bunkyo-ku, Tokyo 112*

*LCC Card No. 85-40413
ISBN 0-8048-1669-7*

*First Tuttle edition, 1991
Second printing, 1992*

Printed in Japan

And the fire and the rose are one.
—T. S. Eliot

Contents

Introduction 9

1 • Everyday Mind Is the Way 17

2 • Everyday Mind: One Is One? 36

3 • Everyday Mind: One Is Two? 52

4 • The Mind of Ambiguity 65

5 • The Center as Other 81

6 • The Center as Mediator 96

7 • The Center: Friend or Foe? 120

8 • Who Can We Turn to for Help? 141

9 • What Do We Need to Know? 165

10 • Arouse the Mind without
      Resting It upon Anything 189

11 • Suffering Suffering 203

Notes 221

Index 239

Introduction

At the top of a one-hundred-foot pole an iron cow gives birth to a calf.[1]

What must we do? Where can we go?

It is when we awaken to the fact that we are, as it were, at the top of a one-hundred-foot pole that we first seriously ask these questions. Life is lived at the frontier of existence, each step a step into the unknown, each moment completely new. But we pretend there is a road of life along which we can walk, that there is an enduring world, and that we can repeat things, that each breath is the same as a previous breath. We pretend all of this in the face of the overwhelming evidence to the contrary, and we make believe that "reality" is an enduring something which goes from the past to the future through the present. Sometimes, however, the road of life collapses into a point, a moment—at the top of a hundred-foot pole. The pretenses break down and we are swept by a vertigo of transience and are filled by a fear of plunging into an abyss of nothing. A moment of true perception, coming from failure, loss, our basic aloneness, or the precariousness of existing, is all that it takes to shatter this complacency about a real enduring world. How often too in life do we arrive at a point where we feel blocked and anxious, where we cannot go forward or backward: as though at the top, as it were, of a hundred-foot pole? "I have to give up," "I can't go on," "I can't make it," "What is the use anyhow?" "Why go on?" "Why bother?" But there is no alternative, life does go on, we cannot give up. Even suicide is its own way of going on.

It is not only individual lives that reach an impasse. Our collective life on earth seems to have reached an impasse of its own. No one needs to be told that we live in very troubled times. From whatever angle we look there are problems and dangers. The technological cornucopia creates one vast heap of waste; attempts to feed the world's populations accelerate soil erosion; our hunger for fuel destroys the quality of our life, while our attempts to preserve that quality of life threaten our survival in an economic world of eat or be eaten; medical discoveries threaten us with overpopulation, and the rapid advances in automation, computers, and electronic gadgetry dazzle us with promises while delivering confusion; the restoration of freedom and dignity to the people of the Third World ushers in the threat of unresolvable inflation with a potential collapse of our financial structure. In the midst of it all, ugly, black, and sinister, are the missiles, pointing to the heart of mankind, but a mere motion of a finger away from homing to that heart with all the consequences that would entail. Something must be done, but what? Where can we go? We have to go forward. We have been rushing downhill on a road to future glory too long to be able to apply the brakes, but is it not just this rushing forward that courts disaster? If we stop the rush long enough to look at our predicament, we find our world poised uneasily, like a huge iron cow on the top of a hundred-foot pole.

How can we get back onto the road of life? We can only hope to change the world if we ourselves are changed. It is of little value to struggle with the world's problems while ignoring our own personal problems, and we cannot put the world right until we have put ourselves right. Each has equal responsibility. If we do not struggle to overcome the war in our own hearts, all the peace conferences, all the marches and demonstrations, protests, and complaints that are made for peace and against war will be to little avail. A big war is, after all, made up of a million small wars that have gone beyond a flash point and spun out of control. The basic issues of our times are the basic issues of each one of us.

The very extreme the world has got to must tell us that the world is not populated by angels called "us" and demons called "them," but by men, women, and children. Each of us has his own pain and confusion, and to blame others, to call upon them to change, to say the world would be a better place without them simply adds to this pain and confusion, theirs and ours. But how do we change ourselves, what is it that must be changed, and what is the Way?

In this book we shall touch on various ways, but Zen Buddhism has been the way followed and practiced by the author for more than twenty-five years. Zen Buddhism originated, according to tradition, when Shakyamuni Buddha, instead of giving a talk, held up a flower before an assembly of monks. Only one monk, Mahakasyapa, understood and smiled. A flower and a smile, a flower that is a smile—this is Zen Buddhism. It is the direct entry into the truth of the world as one vast smile, a living flower. It is far from the gloomy, pessimistic Buddhism that seeks vacancy and is world denying, that was introduced to Europe and America by translators unable to see the truth hidden in the obscurity of style and manner of a culture quite different from their own. Zen is yeasaying. Not in the manner of some hearty optimist, back-slapping and laughing, while calling on everyone to cheer up because things always turn out for the best. Quite the contrary. It is by seeing that all props and reassurances, havens of rest, and harbors from storms are illusory and unnecessary that we awaken to the security of One Mind.

The Zen tradition, because it sees no need to create a bulwark against the erosion of time, has not prized knowledge and learning for its own sake.

Absolute truth, absolute goodness—indeed, any and all absolutes—it regards as symptoms indicating that sickness is in an advanced state. All absolutes can do no more than get us to the top of a hundred-foot pole. The question then is how to take yet another step. Zen Buddhism, therefore, is not a philosophy, theology, or psychology, but a practice. In the practice of Zen one assuages the thirst for the absolute by taking a further step.

This next step is Awakening: the iron cow gives birth. Awakening is the heart of Buddhist practice. "Buddha" means "awakened one" and everyone can awaken. With awakening, the dream of being a separate, isolated individual, with its attendant fear and frustration, fades, while wisdom and compassion, inherent in us all, develop naturally. This has been the message of Zen patriarchs and masters over the past fifteen hundred years.

Most of what is written in this book is based upon experience and observation. If you find something difficult to accept, then it is suggested that you observe yourself rather than try to reason about it from statements made elsewhere in this book or books by other authors. If it is still difficult to accept, then set it aside for the time being. If you find any section particularly difficult, then leave it and return to it later. In a way the whole book should have been written before any chapter was started, and ideally all chapters should be read at once. It would be best, therefore, if at all possible, for you to read the book at least twice.

Quotations have been used freely, not only from Zen sources but from other sources as well. Thus the book is sometimes in the nature of a montage. This kaleidoscopic approach is meant to help the reader summon up the intuitive power to see the whole, the One that can only be pointed toward but not pointed at. In the end the only thing of value is that the iron cow should give birth, even at the top of a hundred-foot pole.

To help in the exposition, koans have been used. Each chapter starts with a koan. A koan is a saying or an action of a Zen master and is an invitation to use the mind in a new way. What this new way is is the subject of the book. As an introduction let us consider the opening koan: "At the top of a one-hundred-foot pole an iron cow gives birth to a calf." In our exposition so far, we have tended to use the koan as a metaphor for the precariousness of our existence. This precariousness comes from two conflicting forces, symbolized by the sterility of iron and the fertility of giving birth: we cannot go on and we have to go on. However, a koan is more akin to irony than to a metaphor. As one writer said, "The essential metaphoric act is a putting together, a synthesis of what had not been united before."[2] One can live with a metaphor, enjoy it, be kept warm by it. But only one taken in by irony would try to live with irony: essentially, irony forces one out. Seeing into irony "is in some respects more like a leap or climb to a higher level than like scratching the surface or plunging down deeper. This leap is always to a higher viewpoint, to a greater vantage point."[3] A koan, like irony, also demands this leap, but not to a new viewpoint.

In the Diamond Sutra it is said that one must arouse the mind without resting it on anything. This is the leap that is required. When a Zen master speaks, he speaks from an aroused mind; to see into the meaning of what he says we must become one with that aroused mind by arousing our own.

The chapters are all held together by the central theme of the dilemma or ambiguity of our condition, and each circles around this ambiguity. The chapters are not strictly consecutive and by and large could be read in any order. Some general guidance might be useful to help readers orient themselves in the book.

The first chapter raises the question "What is the Way?" It comes from a dialogue between two of the most famous Zen masters. It leads into the heart of the matter: that no formula or recipe is possible. It raises the dilemma at the same time it resolves it. The ambiguity of our condition, the causes for it, and the form it takes are discussed most directly in Chapters Two, Three, Four, and Five.

The term *ambiguity* has been used for want of a better word, but the meaning of this term has been taken beyond the ordinary meaning. Ordinarily ambiguity means a two-sided situation: a situation that can equally well be on one side or the other. It is also improperly used to mean vagueness or indefiniteness. My use of the word encompasses the former meaning, but goes one step further in saying that although either side is acceptable, nevertheless one side has to be selected. The implications of this are explored, and it is shown how this ambiguity is the basis of our experience and consciousness at all levels. The "Oneness" that pervades the ambiguity, making two sides unacceptable and forcing us to choose one of them, is shown itself to be ambiguous; while the most fundamental ambiguity is shown to have as one of its faces the fact that there is no ambiguity. This, we will show, is the ultimate irony of life [4]

Human history—social, political, and cultural—no less than the growth of an individual to maturity could be seen as an attempt to come to terms with an ambiguity that demands an ultimate leap if full maturity is to be attained. Without this leap demanded by life, various kinds of "neurotic" solutions are resorted to. Chapters Six, Seven, and Eight broach this neurosis of human growth and show it to be this abortive attempt to resolve the dilemma of existence within existence that creates what is called the ego. Ego is seen to be an illicit union of "uniqueness," "the center," and the "word." The ego is a metaphor for the universe, a metaphor that is taken literally. Chapter Seven discusses the role played by uniqueness and the center, both "standing for" the fundamental Oneness. Chapter Eight discusses the role of language in binding these together, particularly the role of the words "I" and "it" as the mortar of experience and existence.

These chapters point to the need to do something about "ego," and chapters Nine and Ten are concerned principally with this. Chapter Nine is concerned with obedience as one way to struggle with ego, and with the dangers and pitfalls that this way entails. Chapter Ten shows the "structure" of the Mind, the importance of intuition and the intellect, and "knowing" as the basic ground. Some of the less fruitful paths are discussed in the hope that this might help the reader in the search for a Way. The chapter on "Mu!" might, on the face of it, appear to be written for the specialist, for one who is actually practicing. However, this chapter was held in mind throughout the writing of the whole book and is something like the bull's eye of the target.

Finally, the chapter on suffering is an essential element. It would have been good to have placed it at the beginning, or even in the middle, but the structure of the book somehow dictates that it should be at the end. Without taking suffering into account, the book would lack heart.

The book is basically very simple, but unfortunately not easy. If it were made easier it would lose in simplicity and therefore in truth. It may be read at several different levels which address both those who have some acquaintance with Zen Buddhism and those who do not. The layman should not in any way be put off by the use of koans, as these have been used in a way accessible to everyone. The Zen Buddhist, on the other hand, should not be alarmed at their use. The author has struggled with each of them through many long retreats and knows too well their beauty and truth to want to use them other than well.

1
Everyday Mind Is the Way

Joshu asked Nansen, "What is the Tao?" Nansen an-
swered, "Ordinary mind, that is the Tao." Joshu
asked, "Then how do we get onto it?" "The more
you seek after it, the more it runs away," answered
Nansen. Joshu: "If we do not try, how can we know
it is the Tao?" Nansen: "The Tao does not belong to
knowing or not-knowing. Knowing is an illusion;
not-knowing is blank. If you attain to this Tao of
no doubt, it is like vast space. Where is there room
for right or wrong?" At these words Joshu was sud-
denly enlightened.[1]

"What is the Way?" What does this question mean? The
way to where, to what? The way to heaven, the way to
happiness, the way to success? Who is Joshu anyway,
why is he asking this question, and why should it be of
any concern to us?

Joshu was born in China in or about the year AD 778 and died in 898, which would have made him about 120 years old when he died. He was, many feel, one of the greatest Zen masters and one of the great spiritual figures of all time. This koan gives the account of his awakening on his first encounter with his teacher, Nansen. It is said that it took him another twenty-five to thirty years to come to full awakening at the age of about fifty. Joshu worked and studied all this time with Nansen, after whose death he is said to have traveled throughout China to meet with many Zen masters to polish and refine his understanding. At the age of about eighty he settled down and started to teach. There are many stories about Joshu, and all give the impression of a warm, down-to-earth, but subtle teacher.

Perhaps his most famous saying, and the most misunderstood, is: "When I'm hungry I eat, when I'm tired I sleep," which is but another, more concrete way of saying "Everyday mind is the Way.

Nansen (748–834) was also a great teacher. As a student his teachers were Zen masters Nangaku and Baso. He was ordained at the age of thirty and made some considerable study of Buddhist philosophy and disciplinary practice. Among the sutras he studied were the Avatamsaka Sutra and the Lankavatara Sutra, two sutras very much favored among the Zen Buddhists of China, and which will be encountered in different guises throughout this book. One commentator said that Nansen forgot all he knew about Zen when he came to awakening. This is one of those unfortunate statements that can make Zen seem so obscure and impenetrable. It is true that Nansen brought the philosophical teachings of Indian Buddhism down to earth and that this is the most important aspect of his style of teaching; but he did not do away with the philosophy. It is not by destroying the Buddhist philosophy but by bringing this understanding within the orbit of everyday life that Zen has made its great contribution.

Taoism was one of the two great streams of thought that supported and sustained and finally blended with Buddhism to bring about Zen (Ch'an in Chinese). The other great stream was Confucianism. Tao, or the "Way," is a word thoroughly steeped in Chinese philosophy and thought. However, because it was so saturated with tradition and profound thought, it was both a very common and a very loaded word. Even the English word "way" is not simple. It implies "way" as that which is walked or moved along; it also implies the process of walking along. So one could ask, "What is the way to walk the way?" Tao also has the meaning of the Goal: the Way is the Way. Everyday mind is the Way. A monk asked, "What is my treasure?" and the master replied, "Your question is your treasure." This monk was asking, "What is the Way?" The master replied, "Your question is your treasure." In the very seeking and searching is that which is sought after. In the very fact of living is the "way of life."

To help give some idea of how deeply the "Way was embedded in Chinese culture, some quotations are provided below. The approximate dates of the persons concerned are given in parentheses.

> Tung-kuo Tzu asked Chuang Tzu (400 BC), "What is the Way? Where is it?"
> "It is everywhere," replied Chuang Tzu.
> Tung-kuo Tzu said, "It will not do unless you are more specific."
> "It is in the ant," said Chuang Tzu.[2]
>
> Mencius (371 BC) said,
> "The Way is One and only One."
> "The Way is close at hand, but men seek it afar."[3]

Han Fei Tzu (233 BC) said, "The Way is that by which all things become what they are. It is that with which all principles are commensurable. Principles are patterns according to which all things come into being. Tao is the cause of their being."[4]

Huai-nan Tzu (122 BC) said, "The Way covers heaven and supports earth. There is no limit to its height and its depth is unfathomable."[5]

Ho Yen (AD 249) said, "Being, in coming into being, is produced by non-being—that is, Tao in its completeness."[6]

Some writers have likened Tao to the Christian "Logos," which is loosely translated as Word, but also has the connotation of "meaning." Christ has often been called the Logos, the Ultimate Way. "I am the Way, the Truth, and the Life." A Westerner might therefore have asked, had he been Joshu: What is it that has ultimate meaning; or, more simply, what is the meaning of life? We feel we need a meaning or a purpose in life, not some philosophy, but something to work toward, something to look forward to and hope for, some point to life. One of our greatest fears is that we shall find with Macbeth that

> "Life's but a walking shadow, a poor player
> That struts and frets his hour upon the stage
> And then is heard no more. It is a tale
> Told by an idiot, full of sound and fury,
> Signifying nothing."[7]

This fear, no doubt, would have been part of the baggage that Joshu carried with him but which enabled him to put up with the rigors of the journey. Traveling in China in the eighth century must have been arduous: traveling by foot, in all weathers, along rough and broken roads, across swinging bridges, over swollen streams or dizzying canyons, with loneliness, hunger, and sleeplessness as constant companions.

At the end of all that travel Joshu simply asks, "What is the Way?" not "Do you mind if I ask you some questions? There's been a lot going on in my mind just recently and somehow it's all getting me down." Just simply, "What is the Way?" One does not walk hundreds of miles across country in order to ask a philosophical question, but because one is on fire. What is the use of a definition of water when the house is burning down?

Our myths and legends are full of this wandering, searching for the Holy Grail, the Promised Land, the Ring, Moby Dick. One of the oldest, the myth of Gilgamesh, was recorded about five thousand years ago, but it is probably much older even than that. Gilgamesh is said to have traveled to see a teacher and on meeting him to have said, "To see you I have wandered over the world, I have crossed difficult ranges, I have crossed the seas, I have wearied myself with traveling. My joints are aching and I have lost acquaintance with sleep that is sweet. My clothes are worn out. O Father, how shall I find the life for which I am seeking?"[8] Again there is the direct question, "How shall I find the life I am seeking?" How shall I find meaning in my life, what is the Way?

Sri Shankaracharya, the great eighth-century Hindu teacher and reformer, said that a seeker "scorched by the fierce flames of the world forest" addressed his teacher thus: "How shall I cross the ocean of this world? What should be my goal? What way should I take? I know of none. Be gracious, master, save me. Tell me how to end the miseries of earthly life. Withhold nothing."[9]

Joshu said, "What is the Way?" But do not think there is a difference between Gilgamesh, Shankara, and Joshu—or you. Do you say that you do not burn? Then ask yourself: What if life is a tale told by an idiot? What if there is no point to life? If you do burn, then what is one to make of Nansen's reply: Ordinary mind is the meaning; your day-to-day life is the point?

People frequently come to the Montreal Zen Center and say they would like to take up Zen. The question "Why?" is inevitable, and always asked. Some say because their mind wanders and they want to concentrate; some say because they heard it was good for you; some because they are practicing karate or aikido; some because they have read the books of Zen masters and are either intrigued by their iconoclasm, impressed by their independence, or thrilled because it seems so easy. There was one woman who came because she had read a detective novel in which the hero had practiced Zen and was "always so calm and seemed to always know what to do.

But there are some who do not know why. They get fidgety when the question is put and shift about awkwardly on their chair. They look at their hands, look out of the window, sigh, smile, laugh, and sometimes even cry. They are embarrassed. What a strange thing it is to sit dumb or crying, unable to say a single word at a question so obvious and so simple. Is it that they do not know why they want to practice Zen or what they want? Or is it that they know very well what it is, but everything that they can say is not it?

> A monk asked, "What is the correct question and answer?"
> "It is that which one does not speak from the mouth," replied the master.[10]

In fairy stories the fairy often gives the hero three wishes. The first two are spent on wishing for something, and the last on wishing that he didn't have it.

If you ask for peace of mind, concentration, greater understanding, your wish may be granted, only for you to find out too late that that was not what you really wanted. Zen masters never tire of saying that we are "whole and complete and lack nothing."

It is said that Buddha, whose name was Siddhartha Gautama, and with whom Buddhism originated, was born a prince, the son of a rich man, and that at his birth it was prophesied that he would become either a king or a wandering monk. His father wanted his son to follow in his footsteps as a king and did not want him to suffer the privations of an ascetic life. So he did his best to shelter Siddhartha Gautama from the ills and woes of the world, to bury him in pleasures and luxuries, to wall him off from the outside world so that he would have no cause to become a monk.

But the very luxury, comfort, and surfeit of pleasure itself became the goad, and restless with the distraction of distraction, anxious and tired of a life leading nowhere, he broke out from the prison of forgetfulness and entered the blaring world of the town and marketplace. Tradition says he left the palace grounds three times. On the first sortie he met a sick man; on the second, an old man; on the third, a dead man. In a more modern but less concrete idiom, we might say that he became profoundly aware that sickness, old age, and death are constant companions through life. It was these three companions who showed Buddha the Way.

Each of us has these faithful companions attendant upon us always: at breakfast, walking to work, watching TV, in bed. They are there, patient but persistent—cancer, heart attack, stroke, a skidding car, escaping gas, fire, a badly placed ladder. And they do not always come dressed in the heavy boots of war, famine, or disease—there was a newspaper story recently of a man who sneezed and broke his neck.

We can jog, fast, eat vitamins, brown rice, and three different kinds of kelp, but our companions are patient—they'll jog too. We cannot lose them and when the time comes they will be there. Even if, in one's dodging and weaving, sickness misses a punch or two, old age will be there with its toothless (or nowadays, toothy) smile:

> Outliving them all
> Outliving them all.
> Ah! the cold.[11]

And after old age comes death. It is the fact of death that is the goad driving us onward in our search for the Way. A monk said, "I'm not afraid of death." "Then you'll not get far in Zen," was his teacher's reply.

After all of Gilgamesh's journey, after he had pleaded for an end to his suffering, his teacher said, "What endures forever? From the days of old there is no permanence. The sleeping and the dead, how alike they are. The life of man unfolds as he lives: the day of his death is not revealed."[12] Is this not the last thing that Gilgamesh wanted to hear?

When a woman had lost her only child, stung to death by a serpent, she pleaded with Buddha for solace and he promised her solace if she could fetch a mustard seed from a house which had not known death. Is this not fighting fire with fire?

What is the Way? For most the world is a place of exile, through which they wander, longing, longing for home, and everyday life is a pastime or a chore of filling up time. Everything that is encountered raises hopes of home; everything is looked at, examined, from the angle of home: will this be it at last?

> Desolate through forests and fearful in jungles, he is

seeking an Ox which he does not find. Up and down
dark nameless wide-flowing rivers, in deep mountain
thickets, he treads many bypaths. Bone tired, heart-
weary, he carries on his search for this something
which he yet cannot find. At evening he hears cicadas
chirping in the trees.[13]

Show me the way to go home.
I'm tired and I want to go to bed.
I had a little drink about an hour ago
And it's gone right to my head.
No matter where I roam,
On land, on sea or foam,
You will always hear me singing this song,
Show me the way to go home.[14]

My God, my God, why hast thou forsaken me,
Why art thou so far from helping me?

We suffer and cry out. Isolated, misunderstood, alien,
alone, doing a little good, avoiding a little evil, we seem
forsaken by the best. It is as though a light that should be
shining has gone out and we are engulfed in the twilight
of suffering. Life is founded on suffering and suffering
underlies all we do. We suffer because we are hungry
and we suffer because we are full; we suffer because we
have and we suffer because we lack. We suffer because
of love, in fear that we shall lose what we love, and we
suffer when we hate. There is a constant cycle of fear,
hate, greed, boredom, hope, despair. There are, it is
true, bouts of pleasure that come like oases in the desert.
They may be pure and unalloyed, but they cause us
suffering in their very beauty. We come to live in
tomorrow, and tomorrow becomes a disease. We live in
hope; hope sustains us: something to look forward to,
something to grasp. And so by being used and abused,
hope is destroyed. Life may be painful now, we say, but

that is because temporarily things are not quite right. When I get that new job or that new house, my degree, girlfriend, boyfriend, more money, another degree, my life will settle down—calm, serene, and happy. Pain, we believe, is an accident, an intrusion, the bungling of an unthinking fate. We are like people waiting at a railway station for a train that will never come. We await the call that never comes to fulfill a promise that is forever broken. Many die, still waiting.

Our three companions are discreet; they do not block our view, but their shadows are unmistakable: uncertainty, impermanence, and lack. There is always something missing, always something to worry about, always the poignancy of passing time slipping like dry sand constantly and mercilessly through our fingers; with each new decade, a new dread. But even so, behind the dread—glimpsed sometimes as it were, out of the corner of the eye—there is something, some hope, and faith is never quite dead. This something makes itself known through faith in the happy ending, the yearning coming through the strained voices of popular singers, the hope in the lyrics that promise blue skies, pennies from heaven.

Why this faith that there is a way out? Why this constant, even if disguised, search for the way? Why this conviction in so many people that it need not be like this? Why the belief that this bitter life in an alien world is not all, that there is a home, and a way home, even though seen through sugar-coated glasses? What is this echo of a distant haven reverberating, however remotely, through even the most sentimental?

In spite of all the evidence of experience, our own and others, most, if not all of us, are thoroughly convinced that peace and contentment are our true heritage; even though living in misery and despair, we claim that life is not so bad. When Joshu asks, "What is the Way?" he asks

as Everyman, Everywoman, as you and me, and he asks
because he knows deep within that there *is* a way. Is not
the very universality of the search, disguised as it
sometimes may be in the roughest guise, not evidence
that he is right?

When we go to a teacher, we expect good news. No
matter how tedious or grim our life, no matter how
much anxiety, anger, or simple boredom we feel, we
have an instinct that tells us that, if he is really a true
teacher, one who in some measure has realized the
truth, then he'll have tidings of comfort and joy.

It was surely this instinct that supported Joshu as he
stumbled along, burning with thirst for the truth; that
helped him along over those long lonely miles of winter
and struggle. One can imagine him rehearsing his
encounter: now saying this, now that, but always with
Nansen saying the comforting words. But what does
Nansen say?

> Joshu asked, "What is the Way?"
> Nansen said, "Ordinary mind is the Way."

There must have been a long pause after this. The
koan simply goes on to say what Joshu said next, but that
is how a koan is. You have to get right inside it to
understand it. Each koan is talking to you about you
yourself. Just imagine: you are a person for whom life has
unaccountably dried up. There is nothing left to hope
for, yet things as they are just won't do. You feel more
and more desperate and less and less able to acknowledge your desperation. Your everyday life goes on, but
it is like dust and ashes in the mouth. You are only going
through the motions. You are irritable, restless, cannot
concentrate, and cannot divert yourself. Finally you hear
about a Zen master who has all the answers. He lives a
couple of hundred miles away and it will take you a week

or more of hard walking to get to him. Well, I'll do it! If he has the answers, that's where to go. So you pack a few things, take along some money, and walk those miles.

At first the journey is a distraction in itself and you wonder whether it is necessary after all to make this journey: all the problems seem to have left, apart from a blister on each heel. But, after a day or two, it all hits you again, only now much worse. Suppose he doesn't have the answers. Suppose he won't see you. Suppose he dies before you get there. Suppose you can't find him. Hope struggles with despair.

At last you get there, you do find him, he is not dead, he will see you. And then: "What is the Way?" Everyday mind is the Way.

What do you feel? What do you do? He doesn't know the answers. What does he mean? Is he testing me? Does he mean something else? Why doesn't he give a straight answer?

> One day Nansen was working up in the mountains. A monk passed and asked Nansen, "Where does Nansen's Way lead to?" Nansen lifted up his sickle and said, "I bought this for thirty pence". The monk said, "I'm not interested in your sickle that cost you thirty pence. I'm asking you about where Nansen's Way goes to." Nansen said, "I have used it with pleasure and profit."[15]

Disappointment, puzzlement, curiosity, rejection: above all, disappointment. A feeling that the point has gone out of things.

If this man is a Zen master, he is either joking or he means what he says. In Zen it is said that a thousandth of an inch is all the difference between heaven and earth.

If one misses the meaning here, then one misses Zen and one misses life.

It may be as well to pause to see what Nansen did not mean by his "Everyday mind is the Way."

One teacher, commenting upon this koan, said that Nansen meant everyday mind purged of its greed, anger, and ignorance, freed from the bondage of anxiety and pain. But then it is no longer ordinary mind! Or if it is, Joshu's next question would have to be, "How do you purge the mind in this way? How do you get from mind to Mind?" But Nansen is saying mind is Mind. There is no way from mind to Mind. "What is the Way?" means "How do I get rid of all this stuff I carry around with me?"

Some people interpret Nansen to mean that ordinary mind is mediocre mind. They feel that the development and use of any talent or capacity would take them away from "ordinary mind." But for a university professor, ordinary mind is being a university professor, just as being a waiter is ordinary mind for a waiter. A president of a company has the problems of a president of a company. Odd-job people have the problems of odd-job people. Ordinary mind, as Zen master Yasutani-roshi used to say, is "enjoying your riches if you are rich; accepting your poverty if you are poor." Some people say, "I understand what Nansen says but cannot live with this understanding until I am awakened." Do they understand?

Others again will say that if Zen is everyday mind, then there is nothing we need do, nothing we need learn. Spiritual teachers and guides along the way are unnecessary. Some of these will even quote a famous interchange between Zen master Hyakujo and his monks:

"You are a lot of mash eaters," he said, [i.e., one who

eats the leftovers after the juice has been extracted].
"Why do you waste your time going around on pilgrimages? Do you not know that in all the land of
T'ang there is no Zen teacher?" A monk came forward
and said, "But surely there are those who teach disciples and lead communities?" Hyakujo said, "[I know]
I do not say there is no Zen; it is just there are no Zen
teachers."[16]

The monk was stating the obvious, particularly as this
took place during the Tang era, when there were more
Zen teachers than at any other time. Everyone, including
Hyakujo, knew that teachers and communities were
necessary. What does Hyakujo mean then? Is he being
difficult or paradoxical? What is he trying to get across?
     Another Zen master said:

> "I went to my teacher with nothing and came away
> with nothing." Someone asked, "Why bother to go to
> the teacher then?" The reply was, "How otherwise
> would I know that I went with nothing and came
> away with nothing?"[17]

Hyakujo is not putting down Zen teachers, nor the
teaching, nor the monks. He is not saying that religion,
churches, and education have led us to this awful mess.
There is an irony in a teacher talking about teachers the
way Hyakujo does, an irony that is brought out fully by
"I do not say there is no Zen; it is just that there are no
Zen teachers." It is partly from this irony where words
and the situation referred to by the words are in conflict,
that Hyakujo's statement gets its subtle force. In a similar
way Nansen pushes Joshu toward an ultimate conflict by
saying "Everyday mind is the Way." The use of irony in
this way gives an open-ended quality to the teaching that
is given. It is like a gong that is struck and goes on

reverberating. But to truly be one with Hyakujo, one must go on beyond this irony. It is true that "there are no Zen teachers." But in what way is it true? It is true that everyday mind is the way, but how can we see this truth?

A monk went to a teacher to say that he was having trouble with the sutras. The master said, "Don't be upset by the sutras; upset the sutras." He did not say, "Tear up the sutras and throw them away," nor did he say, "Don't bother with the sutras." One's relation to the sutras and with teachers and with everyday mind must be of a particular kind. There has to be an intensely active relation with the teacher—the teacher is a challenge that must be met. But this relation must be based upon deep trust, respect, and gratitude. If this basis of respect and gratitude is there, not only of the student toward the teacher, but also of the teacher toward the student, it is easy to sift, question, doubt, and then respond to the challenge. The more secure the basis, the easier it is to sift, question, and doubt.

In the practice of Zen it is said that one needs great faith, great doubt, and great perseverance to resolve the conflict between these two. The faith necessary is faith in one's own inherent awakened nature and faith in the teacher as a sure guide to that awakened nature. But there is a difference between faith and gullibility.

> A monk asked Tung-shan whether he agreed with all the teachings of his late master.
> "I accept half and reject half," the Abbot said.
> "Why not accept all?"
> "If I did I should be unworthy of my late master."[18]

It is true that teachers abound who prey on the gullibility of a starving population. There have always been those who, when asked for bread, give stones. Every religion has its scribes and pharisees who shut the kingdom of heaven against others because they are afraid to go in themselves. But this does not mean that there is no need for authentic teachers and authentic teachings, or that there are none, or that we should reject all teachers. On the contrary, there has never been a greater need than there is today for authentic people who have gone along the Way and who can light it up for others.

Another fundamental misconception about Zen is that it is a way without effort and exertion, a way without conflict. Such phrases as "doing that is no doing," *wu wei*, "let go" can all lead to the notion that, as one misinformed commentator said, "Zazen is a mini-sabbath in which one relaxes while savoring being rather than doing." Or, as another would have it, "Zazen is sitting quietly doing nothing, allowing an empty but marvelous consciousness to surface."

Far from sparing one conflict, Zen, like true Christianity, pushes one constantly toward conflict: "I bring not peace but a sword," said Christ. "Sustained exertion is not something people of this world naturally love or desire, yet it is the last refuge of all," said Zen master Dogen. Therefore, when Nansen propelled Joshu into everyday mind, he propelled him into a vortex of conflict and confusion.

How many people can tolerate the notion of being ordinary? Yet this, says Nansen, is where you start and end. Many have the hope that spiritual training, Zen, will lift them out of the ordinary round of life, that they will in some measure become extraordinary, unique, or that they will experience extraordinary states of mind, perpetual bliss, a non-stop high. Yet it is precisely this wish that is the first and greatest barrier to true practice. Humility is to accept that one is ordinary, not less or worse than ordinary, but ordinary. The world has known only ordinary people: all our saviors, kings, emperors, presidents, and superstars were and are ordinary.

But this ordinary mind, despised, scorned, and feared, how difficult it is to reach, how easily pushed aside. The ordinary mind is even the mind of judgments, opinions, beliefs, and dogmas. We judge it as bad and look for what is exalted, spiritual, good. This judging it as bad, this search for what is exalted, this search for the way is everyday mind. The "way of everyday mind" is not an easy way.

Dogen said, "It takes sweat, tears, and sometimes blood." Hakuin, a seventeenth-century Zen master, said, "Isn't it strange that everything in the past was so difficult and everything of the present so easy. If the difficulty of the past was good, then the easiness of today is bad. If the easiness of today is good, then the difficulty of the past was bad."[19]

So what does Nansen mean then when he says, "Everyday mind is the Way?" Joshu was also puzzled, because he had to ask, "Then how do we get onto the Way?" Nansen said, "The moment you direct yourself toward it, you go away from it. The more you seek after it, the more it runs away." Do you see what Nansen is doing? Do you see with what a remorseless grip he holds Joshu? He is like a bulldog with massive jaws. Joshu is stymied. Nothing Nansen could say could be plainer, but there must not be so much as a blink of the eye. To practice Zen one must be like a thief in the night, infiltrating without changing a thing. It is like dropping a pebble into a lake without raising a ripple. Joshu is saying: how does one work to realize the truth? And Nansen says even raising a hand banishes the truth forever.

Joshu must have been perspiring by now and comes out with the next question: "If we do not try, how do we know it is the Way?" This is the pivot on which the whole koan turns. It is like a watershed. Nansen is a swordsman who has maneuvered his opponent into a corner: one stumble and it is all over.

If everyday mind is the way—brushing the teeth, going to the bathroom, eating, walking, falling in love, succeeding, failing, getting sick, getting angry, despairing, hoping—if all of this is the way, how can we know it is the way if we cannot make an effort?

The keyword is "know." "How can we know this is the way?" Nansen seizes upon this word and with a stroke of the sword cuts through Joshu's confusion. "The Tao does not belong to knowing or not knowing. Knowledge is an illusion; not knowing is blankness." So if this is so, what then? A student asked Yasutani-roshi, a deeply awakened Zen master, "What is the difference between your touching fire and my touching fire?" Yasutani-roshi said, "No difference at all. Absolutely none! But I know it and you don't."

Someone asked Baso, "What is Buddha?" This is another way of saying, "What is the Way?" Baso replied, "This very mind is the Way." If mind is not concerned with knowing and not-knowing, what is it concerned with? Mind is knowing. There is no way to approach Nansen through an analysis of words and logical structures. To be one with Nansen it is necessary to open the inner eye. Once this eye is opened the truth is everywhere. What is there to know, how can one not know? A fish lives in water, a bird lives in the air. Wherever we look, there it is. A Hindu song says, "My love is in my eyes, that is why I see him everywhere." If the mind is knowing, what is there to know? "If you really attain to this mind of no doubt, it is like the great void, so vast, so boundless. How can there be any division in this mind or Tao?"

The Way is ordinary mind: the argument with a friend, the rebuke from a neighbor, the criticism of a boss. It is like the great void, so vast, so boundless. It is not that first you have the one and then you have the other.

All systems of Buddhist teaching are in the mind, where immeasurable treasures originate. All its supernatural faculties and their transformations revealed in discipline, meditation, and wisdom are sufficiently contained in one's mind and they never depart therefrom. All the hindrances to the attainment of pure knowing which arise from passions that generate karma are originally non-existent. Every cause and effect is but a dream. There is no ordinary world that leaves and no pure knowing to search for. The inner world and the outer mundane world are one and the same. Tao is formless and boundless. It is free from thought and anxiety.

When you have understood this Buddhist teaching you will see there is nothing lacking in you, and you yourself are no different from Buddha.[20]

The only way to come to terms with what Nansen says is by a life-and-death struggle. In this koan is given the way that this struggle must be undertaken. It is no good to go south if the goal lies to the north.

Although Joshu saw into Nansen's mind and became one with him at that moment, nevertheless it took him twenty-five years before he understood what he had seen, and another thirty years before he could call it his own.

2

Everyday Mind: One Is One?

Whenever he was asked a question Gutei simply stuck up one finger. At one time he had a young attendant, whom a visitor asked, "What is the essential point of your master's teaching?" The boy also stuck up one finger. Hearing of this, Gutei cut off his finger with a knife. As the boy ran out screaming with pain, Gutei called to him. When the boy turned his head, Gutei stuck up his finger. The boy was suddenly awakened.

When Gutei was about to die, he said to the assembled monks, "I received this one-finger Zen from Tenryu. I used it all my life but could not exhaust it." When he had finished saying this, he died.[1]

Each koan reveals the whole truth, because the truth is One. Although there are several thousand koans, each can stand by itself. A koan is not like a formula that needs other formulae as supplement and for support. Each koan is a universe in miniature. But what does it mean, that the truth is One? This is what Gutei's finger is about. If we can understand Gutei's action and see into the attendant's finger, we shall see that this koan is the koan of our age, a shattered age searching for unity.

Whenever Gutei was asked a question he would raise a finger: what is the meaning of life? Why was I born? Why must I die? What is God? What is the Devil? What is good? What is evil? Always the same finger came up.

Tradition says that Gutei was alone practicing zazen in the mountains. A nun came upon him and he asked her to rest and have supper with him. She said she would do so if he could say a word of Zen. Gutei was bewildered and didn't know what to say. The nun turned to leave and Gutei said, "It's getting dark, why don't you stay overnight and leave in the morning." The nun turned back and said again, "If you can say a word of Zen, I will stay. If not, I will leave." Again Gutei was unable to respond and the nun left. Ashamed of his inability to respond adequately, Gutei resolved to leave the mountain. However, he had a dream which told him a great master would visit him shortly. A few days later an old monk came by. His name was Tenryu. Gutei told him of his encounter with the nun and asked him for a word of Zen. Tenryu immediately held up a finger and Gutei was awakened.

From this time on, whenever asked a question, Gutei also would raise a finger. But why did he do this? What is the connection between Gutei raising a finger and Tenryu's raising a finger? Are there two fingers—Gutei's and Tenryu's—or one? If two, then is not Gutei simply imitating Tenryu? If one, then how is it we see two fingers?

"It is by the One," said Plotinus, a Greek philosopher of the third century, "that all beings are beings. [If] not a one, a thing is not. No army, no choir, no flock exists except that it be one. No house, even, or ship exists except as the one.

> As one it begets all things, it cannot be any of them—neither thing, nor quality, nor quantity, nor intelligence, nor soul. Not in motion, nor at rest, not in space, nor in time, it is in itself uniform.[2]

Everything is a one, but what of *the* One? "The One is absent from nothing and from everything. It is present to all those who can touch it and absent only to those who cannot. We are not separate from the One nor distant from it. It is because of the One that we breathe and have our being."[3]

This One has haunted humanity from the very beginning. How can so many be one? Are the ones—chairs, ships, ourselves—also the One? "That which is One into all hath developed."[4] Thus it was said in the Vedic hymns, hymns as old as history. Again, from these same hymns: "There was not then what is nor what is not. There was no sky, and no heaven beyond the sky . . . The One was breathing by its own power, in infinite peace. Only the One was: there was nothing beyond. Darkness was hidden in darkness. The all was fluid and formless. Therein, in the void, by the fire of fervor, arose the One."[5]

This "One" is the subject of all Zen koans.[6] Each koan in its own way comes out of and leads to this One. Some emphasize Oneness as "no self," emptiness, or boundless totality without content. Others emphasize the immediacy of Oneness as dynamic presence. Some emphasize not-twoness, and others emphasize perfect interpenetration. However, it is simply a difference of emphasis. All koans fall to some extent in all four classes and many defy classification. The only reason these classes are mentioned is to bring out that the Oneness of Zen is not a static, numerical One, nor a flaccid, total collection of all that is.

We yearn for Oneness while being the One we yearn for. As Zen master Hakuin says, we are "like one in water crying 'I thirst'; like a child of rich birth wandering poor on this earth we endlessly circle" trying to find the One that we are.

> He who is in the Sun and in the Fire and in the heart of man is One. He who knows this is one with the One.—Hindu
>
> Hear, O Israel, the Lord our God, the Lord is One! —Hebrew
>
> No divinity if not One divinity.—Mohammed
>
> The entire universe is one bright pearl.—Gensha
>
> One fist is the entire universe.—Dogen
>
> There exists just the One Mind.—Huang Po
>
> I and the Father are One.—Christ
>
> Above the heavens, below the heavens, I alone am the Honored One.—Buddha
>
> The way is one and only One.—Mencius

Hear, O Israel, the Lord thy God, the Lord is One! What a revelation, what an awakening is this. Gone are the shadows of confusion and multiplicity arising from a patchwork world of tribal gods and demons; gone is the obscurity of magic and superstition. The Lord thy God is *One.* Is not this call the beginning? Not the beginning in time, but the beginning that is always present. Is not this One the Light of the world? Not the light that is only seen, but the light that is heard, smelt, tasted, and touched. Hear, O Israel: the clarion call that awakens the dead, the dead that are raised by raising a finger.

The Lord thy God is One: if not unity, then no divinity.

If not One, there is no god. The divine is One and religion is the celebration of Oneness, the celebration of Light. Light and life are One: not the light of day nor the life opposed to death, but the Light of Life. "I am the Way, the Truth, and the Life." "I and the Father are One." "Throughout heaven and earth, I alone am the Honored One." Mohammed too raised a finger—Mohammed, Buddha, and Christ—one voice: Hear, O Israel, the Lord thy God is One.

This One is in the heart of man and in the heart of lions and horses, tigers and cows, cats, rats, and bats. No, not *in* the heart, but *is* the heart. "He who is in the sun, and in the fire, and in the heart of man, is One. He who knows this is one with the One."[7] If faith, then faith. If one, then One.

What is this One that is now called God, now the heart of man, now revealed in a single finger? When Gutei raised his finger, what did he have in mind? Does he mean the finger is a symbol for the One? Or is it a metaphor, the finger stands for the One, or the finger is like the One? But if so, why did he cut off the attendant's finger? If the finger is simply pointing to Oneness or standing for Oneness, is not the attendant's finger as good as Gutei's? Was the competition too much? Were there two fingers instead of one and one had to go? Suppose Gutei's assistant had raised two fingers, or five fingers—how many would Gutei have had to cut off then?

One fist is the entire universe, said Zen master Dogen. One fist! Raising the fist was the fascist salute.[8] How then can one fist be the entire universe? Or is there a difference between Hitler's fist and Dogen's?

> Above the heavens and below the heavens, I alone am the Honored One.—Buddha
>
> It is I who am God, no other apart from me.—Jehovah
>
> I am, none else beside me.—Hitler

Is it just a quirk of language that makes Hitler and Buddha, Hitler and Jehovah, sound so much alike?

Surely it is a mistake to look for the origin of religion in questions such as "What is man?" "What is the meaning of existence?" "What is good and evil?" Religion does not come from questions, but comes from a voice crying out in the wilderness, from the voice of the One crying for the One. Stifle the voice and the rocks and stones would cry out. Religion is the opiate of the masses, said Marx.[9] God, said Freud, is but a surrogate father.[10] Here at two more voices: the one crying for heaven called utopia, the other crying for God called reason. But religion is not supplanted by utopias nor is it dethroned by reason. Nor, moreover, is it necessarily the search for the good.

Religion in the West has for so long been associated with a search for good that the evil in religion has been overlooked. "That evil can appear in the shape of light, of good deeds, of historical necessity is plainly confusing to someone who comes from our traditional world of ethics,"[11] because we think the One *has* to be good. "Religion," said Alfred North Whitehead, a celebrated philosopher, "is by no means necessarily good. It may be very evil."[12]

> Christ said, "The Father and I are one."
>
> Hitler said, "I am Germany, Germany is me."

Each proclaims One where others would proclaim two. "One Church, one faith, one God," the Roman Catholic Church says in effect. "One Reich, one Volk, one Führer," said Hitler.

A group of German Protestants published a manifesto in 1933 recognizing the danger of this new religion. "We see our people threatened by a mortal danger. The danger is that of a new religion."[13] But at the same time others were enthusiastic and "as storm troopers of Jesus Christ" wanted to organize the German Evangelical churches and bring the Protestants in line with the Nazi regime. These people said, "The eternal God created for our nation a law that is peculiar to its own kind. It took shape in the leader, Adolf Hitler. One nation! One God! One Reich! One Church!"[14]

Was Hitler engaging in some Satanic black mass, usurping the power and strength of two thousand years' faith? Was he simply a fake imitating that which he could not even begin to understand? Was Gutei's assistant a fake, imitating something he could not begin to understand? Then the koan would be a rather pointless story about a master chastising a student. But one sweep of the knife and the assistant was free. This suggests that the student was close to something before the knife flashed, that he saw that all was one and was indicating this when he raised his finger. What was wrong, then, in his raising it? "One fist is the entire universe." Can that fist be lopped off?

The entire universe is one bright pearl—perfect, whole, and complete. This pearl, that Christ called the pearl of great price, is it not the One Mind? Huang Po said, "When all the Buddhas manifest themselves in the world, they proclaim nothing but the One Mind." Nothing but the One bright pearl. Without a flaw—luminous, smooth, pure, and peerless—the One Mind knows no second. So where does Hitler come in, where do the S.A., the S.S. find a place in the serenely shining and peerless pearl of great price?

Zen master Shibayama said, "Oneness can only be achieved by hard training." Zen master Yasutani said, "If you think, then your precious life of Oneness will be destroyed." What is this Oneness? How can the One Mind, which knows no second, be achieved only by hard training and how can it be lost by thinking? How can

Oneness be achieved? If it is achieved, is it Oneness? If it is lost, where will it go? Are Shibayama-roshi and Yasutani-roshi then mistaken? But if they are, then there is no difference between Buddha and Hitler. Buddha is One, Hitler is One. But who would want to aver this "no difference"? Yet if there is a difference, then is there a difference too between Buddha and Christ, between Christ and Mohammed, between Mohammed and Dogen? Hear, O Israel, the Lord thy God is . . . how many? If the One is many, why should Hitler not be the One?

For years religion has been buried deep beneath the debris of wars and the aftermath of prosperity and waste; for the sceptical and indifferent the religious institutions of the world have lost their place as a bulwark of society and have become tourist attractions at best, bingo parlors at worst. But if religion is the celebration of Oneness, can it ever really die? The One will not perish for how can life die? If religion cannot be clothed in ermine and crowned with a miter, then it will make do with a black shirt and steel helmet. If we cannot have a patriarch or saint, then we will put up with a wretched tramp from some Austrian flop house, strutting with fist raised before hundreds of thousands of worshipers, calling out in a raucous voice, "I am, none else beside me," proclaiming a religion of Oneness, alias order, at all costs. In our craving for Oneness, we grasp for even a counterfeit One, although it is still the One that grasps.

Can this One be experienced? If not, how can we talk about it? If so, what is it that is experienced? Or perhaps it is just an abstraction. After all, an abstraction is something that can be thought about but not experienced. But then, wherein lies the power of Oneness to move? Philosophers and artists have sought for this Oneness as men dying in the desert search for water. Some have died in the quest, some have gone mad, some have committed suicide. And for an abstraction? If truth is a simplifying idea that magically transforms a mosaic of theory and fact into an elegant whole, if beauty is a harmony of parts that allows each to give and receive from a whole, what is this whole? Is it not but another name for the One? Whole and complete means One and nothing left outside. Although a philosopher may express the One abstractly and incompletely, it does not mean that that which relentlessly drives the philosopher to his search is abstract and incomplete.[15]

Oneness is not an abstraction—not simply a way of summing up thoughts and ideas, a logical extension of the tendency of the mind to generalize. Even power and its cultured brother, authority, are but children of the One Hand clapping, whose silence is so thunderous that the roar of the bombs and the bullets of all wars put together makes not even a muffled echo.

A mighty fortress is our God; but what is this mysterious fortress that none can assail or destroy, this source of miracles, magic, science and superstition, wonder and war? Can you count the galaxies, compute the stars, imagine their planets, breathe in the unbelievable number of atoms in all of this, and put it all into one finger—and then say that the One is an abstraction?

A monk asked Joshu, "If all return to the One, to what does the One return?"

Some say that Gutei's assistant did not know much and was a mere boy, imitating, perhaps even conditioned by, his teacher. This would mean that Gutei was merely rebuking the boy and, in severing the boy's finger, accidently brought him to awakening. But Zen masters are not disciplinarians, rebuking in order to teach. If the boy is a mere imitator, what value has the koan? If the boy is conditioned, what value has Zen?

What if the assistant were not some beginner? What

if, on the contrary, he was an advanced student, so much so that it took only one sharp shock to bring him to awakening? What if this awakening, moreover, is worth a finger or an arm, or even life itself? It would not then have been an accident.

Gutei's assistant saw the One as one finger; Gutei severed the finger. The head monk (referred to in Hui-neng's autobiography) saw the One as a bright mirror. Hui-neng smashed the mirror. From the beginning, not a thing is, not even the One. Thou shalt not make a graven image, . . . and yet we do just this, or have others do it for us, sometimes with ghastly consequences. A fraction of an inch is all the difference between heaven and hell, or the Third Reich.

Just as there are those who would dismiss Gutei's assistant and the head monk as of no consequence, as two who had no real understanding, so most would want to dismiss Hitler as some ridiculous clown, strutting across the world stage left vacant for a moment by the true heroes of history. As tramps with ridiculous moustaches and an idealism perverted by a world of matter, he and Charlie Chaplin seemed to be twins: mirror images of the ridiculous reflecting the absurd. And so we laughed at the Great Dictator who, meanwhile, with a massive power never before equaled, crushed Europe.

Instead of being called ridiculous, Hitler was then called mad—a madman surrounded by idiots like Goering, fanatics like Himmler, and ignoramuses like Goebbels. He and his entourage were mad, it was said. Indeed, some would have it that the whole German nation was mad. Humanity wanted to cut off its German arm to save its soul. If the Germans are mad, we do not have to worry. God is good and all's well with the world.

If it were *Germans* that slaughtered Jews and plundered the Russians, then, if we can say the Germans are mad, we can avoid the guilt. But if it is human beings killing human beings, brothers slaughtering brothers, the self plundering the self, then the whole world might be the nightmare of a madman. Who could tolerate that vision?

A panel of psychologists conducted a series of personality tests upon the German defendants at the Nuremburg trial of war crimes. They were to produce a report, but the report never appeared. One member of the panel suggested that the reason it did not appear was that "the results did not reveal what everyone expected, even required, that they reveal: that the Nazis were demented creatures. What they did in fact reveal was that such personalities are not unique or insane (and) could be duplicated in any country of the world today."[16]

Some people called Hitler mad, some said he was a Messiah, the incarnation of Oneness: "His never-to-be-forgotten words affected me as the words of a prophet."[17] "The Sun shone all the time he was there."[18] "My belief is that our leader, Adolf Hitler, was given by fate to the German nation as our savior bringing light to darkness."[19] "The Führer's act (which led to the murder of thousands of his closest followers) is not subject to the dispensation of justice for it was itself the highest form of justice."[20] "He spoke less to the people's political convictions than to their spiritual state."[21] A Hamburg school mistress was one among many of the people who "had witnessed scenes of moving faith which showed Hitler as the helper, rescuer, redeemer from our overwhelming need."[22] Nietzsche's sister said Hitler struck her as being a religious leader rather than a political leader.[23]

In the light of history, we know that some awful calamity occurred, a calamity stunning in its proportions. But what happened? Why did a civilized country follow him and even men of the stature of Heidegger support him?

Madman or prophet, buffoon or messiah, he must have struck some chord deep in the hearts of people. There must have been something beyond all the ranting and raving, the obscene and the spurious. If not, how are we to understand him?

What was extraordinary about Hitler was the speed with which everything was accomplished. It is this speed and the enormity of what evolved that shows the power of Oneness in human affairs. About 1920 Hitler entered politics: an unknown man who ten years earlier had been a tramp. He had no connections, no education, and no money. In twenty-one years he had established supreme control over the German people and had an empire that covered Europe from France through Belgium, Holland, Denmark, Norway, half of Russia from Leningrad to Stalingrad, Hungary, Austria, Poland, Czechoslovakia, Greece, Rumania, Yugoslavia, Crete, and North Africa from El Alamein to Tunisia. Oneness is the supreme catalyst. It is like the wind that blows where it will. It is this that gives the key to understanding prophets as well as demagogues. The speed with which Hitler accomplished everything is a property of catalysis. For example, take oxygen and hydrogen and a flash of energy and there is water. It is like the eruption of an idea. At one moment there is confusion and concern, and the next everything is clear and in order. This flash of insight, of energy, is Oneness at work.[24] "Hitler's catalyzing powers were indispensable and everything: the will, the goal, the cohesion, instantly disappeared without the physical presence of Hitler (after his death)."[25]

Unity: Oneness. The lust for "purity of blood," the abhorrence of racial mixture, the crushing insistence upon one party, upon loyalty, upon world conquest.

How are we to understand this—as madness, as magic, as misplaced sexuality, as a historical accident?

The human being is a religious being, a being at home only in Oneness, and religion is not necessarily good.[26] The One Mind will always out, even if it is the mind of the devil. "The devil too is One."

A well-known writer has said, "Because there is One Mind there can be no evil." But because there is wood, can there be no dark wood as well as light? Black is black, white is white, gray is gray, through and through. To say that One Mind is good only and evil but an illusion is not only denying One Mind; it is also dangerous.

Hitler was not an isolated phenomenon, nor the first to proclaim himself the Messiah. Mankind has been pursuing the millennium throughout history, before and since the birth of Christ. History is studded with stories of the coming of the Son of Man and of His being identified with this or that man destined to bring heaven to earth. Hinduism is impregnated with the myths of the avatar, and the Hero has a thousand or ten thousand faces.

Recently an American history teacher conducted a course involving the Nazi era.[27] The students, following a film showing Nazi atrocities, said that the fault lay with the German people and such a thing could never happen in America. The teacher, wanting to show the dynamics involved, conducted an experiment to show the methods and motivations of the Nazis. With the agreement of his class he introduced vigorous discipline, immediate response without thought, preferably of the yes-and-no variety, and unthinking obedience. He removed ambiguity and disorder, replacing them with certainty and security. As did the Nazis, he introduced symbols, slogans, and salutes, so that the class could identify with each other, the "movement," and the leader. After a while, when the movement had taken hold, he claimed it was part of a greater movement that was leading Americans toward a more simple and orderly life based upon ideals of humanity and goodness. It is not difficult to see that below the surface of his actions he was arousing order, unity, identity, belongingness, togetherness—in a word, he was arousing Oneness. Order, pattern, structure, meaning, purpose are all ways Oneness manifests.

The teacher wanted the "experiment" to be a short one and just sufficient to give a vicarious taste of Nazism. To his amazement the Movement, which was called the "Wave," spread out from his class across the campus. More and more students became involved, shedding their individuality to become part of a greater whole which, as it grew, increased in attraction.

As it grew some of its members became more and more fanatical in their adherence to the Movement and those who were not interested found themselves ostracized, and minority groups began to suffer. In the end the school authorities became alarmed at the monster that was growing in their midst and it was decided the experiment should be called off.

In order to bring the experiment to an end in such a way as to bring home his point, the teacher, who was now ostensibly the local leader of the Wave, called a mass rally, which had all the characteristics of a miniature Nuremberg rally. He said that at the meeting the members would see their national leader—and they did. After allowing tension, expectation, and hope to increase to a point, the teacher suddenly flashed a photograph of this leader on a large screen. It was a picture of Adolf Hitler.

Gutei's finger is the koan of our age. Our world is troubled, in conflict, dangerous. As we struggle to digest Buchenwald, Auschwitz, gulags, Vietnam, and the Middle East, we tense up, awaiting the next disaster. In the chaos and confusion we yearn for unity; we long for it so much that we run the risk of accepting it at any price and of being led astray to a Oneness of isolation and alienation, to a religion of destruction and despair, as did the ill-fated Germans only a few decades ago. On one hand there is the Oneness of Gutei, on the other, that of his assistant. On one hand there is Buddha, on the other there is Hitler. How is it that there are two? These are not idle questions, but the very substance of the koan. Why did Gutei cut off the finger and what did the attendant "see" that brought him to awakening? Another way of asking this same question is, "How would the attendant respond if someone were to ask him about the fundamental principle after his finger had been cut off?"

"Because there is One Mind there can be no evil." This will not do. Gensha, a Zen monk, said, "You know, even in the black mountain of demons, freedom is working." Bodhidharma said, "The holy and the profane are of one essence."

"While he was washing his bowl a master watched two crows fighting over a frog. A monk came up to him and asked, 'Why should they reach such a state?' The master replied, 'It is simply because of you.'"[28] Me? Why is there so much struggle and conflict in the world? Why must there be Hitlers, Himmlers, and Stalins?

Conflict must come from two opposing principles. The two crows each see themselves as the One, just as Gutei's assistant would see himself as the One. But on the other hand, if Oneness is basic, why should this conflict appear? "It is because of you," said the master. To whom is he referring?

Buddha said, "Whoever sees me by form, perverted are his footsteps upon the Way." Jesus said, "It is I who am the light which is above them all. It is I who am the All. From me did All come forth and unto me did all extend. Split a piece of wood and I am there. Lift up a stone and you will find me there."[29] From the One comes all and I am that One. I am the crow and the frog, the storm trooper and his victim. I am the One who is in the sun and in the fire and in the heart of man. The One who knows this is one with the One.

Oneness is sometimes called in Buddhism the "Buddha nature." Zen master Yasutani, commenting upon Buddha nature, said, "What is the substance of Buddha nature? In Buddhism it is called Ku (Shunyata). Now Ku is not mere emptiness. It is that which is living, dynamic, devoid of mass, unfixed, beyond individuality or personality—that matrix of all phenomena. It is here we have the fundamental principle or doctrine or philosophy of Buddhism."[30]

A Zen master said, "From the beginning not a thing is"—no swastika, no gas chamber, no Fuhrer. Nothing has a self nature: everything is One Mind. If we think there is a finger, it will sooner or later be chopped off, blown off, or burnt off. But if we insist on this "no finger," then we fall into a pit deeper than hell. It is not a question of emptying the mind, but of seeing into the emptiness of mind: even a mind full of hate is empty. A Zen master said, "There is a type of man who intentionally searches for the void through abiding in stillness. His understanding is the opposite of truth." "When the utmost void is reached, awakening is still not obtained. It is only when one is clear as the morning that the Unique One can be seen."[31] If we can understand this, we will understand what the attendant saw after his finger had been cut off.

There is something both innocent and innocuous about Gutei raising his finger, but when he does the whole world shifts on its axis.

3

Everyday Mind: One Is Two?

*Goso asked a monk, "Sei and her soul are separated—
which is the true person?"*
　　*The story of Sei's two souls appears in various Chi-
nese books of ghost stories and is as follows: "In a
place called Koyo lived a man, Chokan, whose young-
est daughter, Sei, was very beautiful, and the pride of
her father. She had a handsome cousin named Ochu
and Chokan as a joke used to say they would make a
fine married couple. The two young people, however,
took this chaffing seriously, and thought of themselves as engaged, being in love with each other. The
father, however, intended to give Sei in marriage to
another young man, Hinryo, and tragedy could not
be avoided. In indignation Ochu left the place by
boat, and after several days' journey, found one evening, to his astonishment, that Sei was on the same
boat. Overjoyed, they went to the country of Shoku
where they married and later had two children. Sei,
however, could not forget her native place, and feeling she had deserted her father, wondered what he
was thinking of her. She longed to return so her husband decided to go back with her. When they arrived
Ochu left Sei at the port and went to the father's
house to apologize to the father for taking his daughter away from home, and to beg him for forgiveness
"What is the meaning of all this?" exclaimed the fa-*

ther, "Who is this woman you are talking about?" "It is Sei," replied Ochu. "Nonsense!" said Chokan. "After you left Sei became ill and was in bed for several years. That's not Sei at all!"

Ochu went back to the boat, and brought Sei to her father's house. Being told of this, the Sei lying in bed, when the Sei came from the boat, arose from her bed and went toward her, and the two became one. Chokan said that after Ochu had left, his daughter never spoke, and lay there as if in a stupor. The soul must have gone from the body. Sei said that she had not known her body was in the house. When she felt Ochu's love, and saw him go, she had followed him as in a dream, but after that had remembered nothing.[1]

Sei and her soul are separated.

If Oneness is basic, how is twoness possible? This is the most fundamental of all mysteries: if God is good, how is it that evil exists; if I am whole and complete, why do I suffer? Buddha said, "Throughout heaven and earth, I alone am the Honored One": are other people then simply imaginary? If Oneness is basic, where do conflict, suffering, war, and pain come in? Can Oneness be Oneness if it is divided against itself? Is the search for unity an illusion, like the crock of gold at the foot of a rainbow? Or is the belief in diversity and multiplicity the illusion? If there is just One Mind, does this One Mind know? If so, what does it know; if not, why call it Mind?

Sei is an individual and the word individual means indivisible. Do you think the story far-fetched? Then consider the following: Bunuel, the late Spanish film director, directed the film "Cet Obscur Objet de Désir," in which a man tries to seduce a woman, Conchita—not an unusual plot. For a short while all seems to go well for him, then at the critical moment Conchita changes completely and instead of welcoming and encouraging his advances, she repulses him. Then, when all seems lost, she again becomes compliant and seductive. This is still nothing new. What makes the film different is that *the role of Conchita is played by two entirely different actresses:* the compliant one by one actress, the reluctant one by another. The two actresses are not at all alike in appearance, speech, or mannerisms. Yet what is interesting is that Bunuel, with very clever direction, manages to maintain the illusion that there is just one person, *one girl played by one actress.* Not until the film is two-thirds through does one awaken to what is happening, when the spell is broken to let the viewer in on the secret that two different actresses are involved in playing one role. But which one of the two is the true Conchita?

Goso asked a monk, "Sei and her soul are separated; which is the true person?" This same twoness in one person is brought out in a quotation from the Gnostics of the first and second centuries, who had profound affinities with both Buddhism and Christianity:

> I am the first and the last. I am the honored one and the scorned one. I am the whore and the holy one. I am the wife and the virgin. I am [the mother] and the daughter. . . . I am she whose wedding is great and I have not taken a husband.[2]

Which is the true person?

Another example from fiction is that of Dr. Jekyll and Mr. Hyde, a character from R.L. Stevenson's famous novel of the same name: on the one hand a gentleman and compassionate doctor, on the other a demon and heartless murderer.

Observe another carefully and you will see two people. One is an affable, gentle person, friendly perhaps, somewhat weak, and even sentimental, kind to others; this person has a bright, smiling face and is easily accessible. The other is hard and businesslike, dedicated to getting things done, cold, somewhat insensitive; efficient in a way, but difficult to get to, difficult to understand. The two are not always obvious, sometimes the one is reserved for home, the other for the office, but these two are always subtly there. Look at a full-face photograph of this person and what do you see? Cover the left side, now the right side. Is there not a difference?

When Eichmann, responsible for the administrative aspects of the systematic destruction of much of European Jewry, appeared on the stand in an Israeli court, it was hard to reconcile the somewhat docile, slightly deaf, and puzzled-looking man, who it was said loved his family and was particularly fond of dogs, who believed in God and prayer, with the fiend described by one after another of the surviving victims of his pitiless reign.

Which was the true Eichmann? Which the true Conchita? Which is the true Sei? Indeed, which is the true you? Don't you have this eternal struggle between sensuality and sainthood? Don't you feel that whatever you are doing you ought to be doing something else? Do you yourself not have these strange contradictions, perhaps wanting to be at the center and wanting to retire into the background at the same time? Or wanting to live a pure life and wanting to kick over the traces? Or wanting a full and busy life, but wanting a life of solitude and quiet?

This is what the koan is about: twoness and oneness—two women, one Sei. The question then arises whether these two have to be made into one. If so, what is this one? If not, which is the true Sei? The one who went into the world and had a husband and children? Or the one who remained a recluse, retiring, silent, and turned inward?

This koan is not about mere duality or the coexistence of two ways of being, two personalities in one body, or two complexes within a single mind. The koan is not asking which should triumph, Sei or her soul, Dr. Jekyll or Mr. Hyde, the nun or the whore. It is talking about two equal and valid ways of being, neither of which can triumph over the other nor merge with the other. If Sei is an individual, which is the individual?

The problem pointed up in the koan does not simply belong to Sei, Eichmann, or Dr. Jekyll. It is universal. It is the problem of each of us. Furthermore, it is not a psychological one to be resolved by therapy: its universality involves the universe itself, and as such it is a religious problem. If we fail to see this one/two contradiction as the fundamental problem of religion, we can never find a secure basis for our life and will forever build upon shifting sands. Sei is Everywoman, Everyman, and we must see into this koan or miss the point of art, religion, Zen, and even life itself.

To see into the koan we must see *into* ourselves. It is *in* ourselves that we can see clearly the dimensions of this question: is it one or is it two? Let us not be too hasty with our conclusion.

A Zen master was washing his bowls and watching two crows fighting over a frog. A monk came up to him and asked, "Why should they reach such a state?" The reply was, "It is simply because of you."

Before going on, it is interesting to note parenthetically that modern theoretical physics has its own Sei in the form of light, which is now a particle, now a wave, depending upon the kind of experiment conducted.

Neils Bohr, one of the great physicists of our time, proposed a principle of complementarity, which would provide an epistemological basis for accepting this indeterminacy. This principle would accept twoness as fundamental. Einstein could not agree and bluntly said so at a congress of physicists in 1911. Einstein was convinced of oneness and could not accept twoness. "Then the discussion opened out. Lorentz did his best to give the floor to only one speaker at a time. But everyone felt strongly. Everyone wanted to put his own view. There was the nearest thing to an uproar that could occur in such distinguished company."[3] The debate still goes on in physics: Is it one, is it two?

This reminds one of the case tried before a judge who said, after hearing the case for the prosecution, "You're quite right!" The counsel for the defense hurriedly put forward his case. "You're quite right!" said the judge. The clerk of the court leapt up, somewhat hot under the collar, and said, "M'lord, they can't both be right." "You're quite right!" said the judge. Einstein is quite right: God does not play dice, there is no ambiguity in oneness. Bohr is quite right: twoness is fundamental, the world is basically ambiguous.

In spite of the above digression, this problem of oneness/twoness is fundamental and basic to human nature, so basic in fact that wars have been fought, and are likely yet to be fought, because of it. To see it simply as a philosophical or theological dispute would be to miss the point.

A monk asked a master, "When a snake swallows a frog, should you save its life or not?" To save its life you kill the snake; not to save its life is to leave the frog to die; and yet each has the right to life. A similar dilemma is faced in the question of abortion and birth control. In life we have to act: even inactivity is its own form of action.

In order that we can refer to this oneness/twoness in

a more elegant fashion, let us call it *ambiguity,* or the *ambiguous.* This word is very apt, being itself ambiguous, as its root *ambi* means both one and two.

On the one hand, the word *ambit* means the totality of space in which an action may take place. *Ambience* means the unity underlying the subtle interpenetration of influences. *Ambition* is that which unifies desire, dreams, intentions, and actions. It is a univalent thrust. *Ambi,* therefore, means oneness.

On the other hand, the word *ambivert* means going in two opposite directions. Sei is an ambivert in that she is both introvert (one who turns inward) and extrovert (one who turns outward). *Ambivalent* means to be both attracted to and repelled by something. Conchita, for example, was ambivalent toward her lover and his advances. *Ambidextrous* means to be able to use both hands equally well. So *ambi* has the meaning of both or two.

This justification for the use of the word *ambiguous* in the way it is being used here—for which the author is indebted to Leonard Bernstein's lectures on music—is not insisted upon. We are using a word to designate a situation which has so far not been isolated as such, and *ambiguous* seems the least objectionable.

Unfortunately ambiguity has acquired a further meaning—that of "vagueness." A figure half seen in the twilight might be called ambiguous. In this book, the figure would be considered ambiguous only if it is seen now as a woman, now as a rock or a tree.

In the particular sense in which we are using the word, ambiguity means: "Is it one, is it two?" If it is one, it cannot be two. If it is two, it cannot be one. But it also means, if it is two, which of the two is it: is it Sei *or* is it her soul; is it Dr. Jekyll *or* Mr. Hyde? Are you the affable one or the hard one, both, or neither? Who are you? What are you? It is confusing, but the confusion after all has a structure—a confused order, an orderly confusion at that.

Consider Figure 1. Is this a picture of a young lady or an old lady?

Figure 1

If it is a young lady, then the old lady disappears; if an old lady, then the young lady disappears. Can it be said that it is *either* one *or* the other? Would it make sense to say the young lady is real and the old an "illusion"? Each picture has equal claim, does it not? However, we cannot say that it is both a young lady and an old lady because *when we see the one we do not see the other.* Nor can we say that it is neither a young lady nor an old lady. Which is the true lady, the young or the old? Which is the true Sei?

Sei and her soul are parted. It is no good theorizing as

to which is the true Sei. The koan calls for an immediate response, not an explanation. It is a concrete problem: which is the true Sei? Explanations simply give the dimensions of the problem, they cannot help resolve it. The world is divided into East and West—which is the true world? America is divided—liberal, Democrat, conservative, Republican. Which is the true America? Canada is divided, Britain is divided. Which is the true Canada, the true Britain?

India at the time of its independence in 1947 gave a truly painful example of this. Gandhi wanted India to retain the political, economic, and traditional integrity of India and felt that India could and should live with its religious duality of Moslem and Hindu. Others, however, notably Jinnah, the Moslem leader, insisted that there should be religious unity at the cost of economic and political duality. Mountbatten had to decide which was the true India, the economic or the religious.

Life is basically ambiguous, but so often it demands, as does this koan, a single unambiguous response. Poised on the horns of the dilemma "to be or not to be," am I or am I not, unable to move forward and unable to go back, unable to will one thing, unable to commit ourselves unequivocally, but unable to finally withdraw—our life is frustrating and painful, full of the feeling of wasted opportunities and of being taken in when we would rather do otherwise.

The ambiguity of freedom is one example among many of the ambiguities of life.[4] There are few words as heavily charged as this word *freedom*. Countless men and women have died for "freedom," and every person has or will pass the "barrier" in life between childhood and adulthood where freedom becomes an issue. But what is freedom? We can be sure that the next war will be fought in its name, as were the myriads of wars of the past. Revolutions erupt in the name of freedom:

freedom, equality, and brotherhood: *liberté, egalité, fraternité*. But if Americans fight Russians for freedom, will not the Russians fight the Americans for the same cause? What is freedom and what is the opposite of freedom? Although many people might have difficulty with the first question, the second can be answered readily. Bondage is the opposite of freedom. Or is it?

As a child grows up he or she wants to be free and so rebels. "I want to do as I like without your interference. I want to make my own mistakes. I'm not like you and in any case things are different now from when you were my age." But freedom is not all that children want. They also want security. The world is wide and vast and can be very threatening. So often a child breathes a sigh of relief when arriving home after some particularly risky enterprise, feeling the security, warmth, and certainty of being home. But how soon does this security become a burden?

The logical opposite to freedom may be bondage, but in experience the opposite of freedom is security and *security is as desirable as freedom.* Often, however, the price of one is the loss of the other. It is the security/freedom dilemma, with the overtones of "Am I a child or an adult?" "Can I cope or can't I?" "Am I or am I not?" that makes the struggle of the teenager so fierce. "I have to opt for one or the other, but if I opt for the one I cannot opt for the other—and I want both."

It is not only teenagers that struggle like this. A feminist writer explores this same dilemma and shows that women have as a group opted for security over freedom and have consequently, to a considerable degree, voluntarily sacrificed freedom. The struggle in the liberation movement therefore is as much a struggle with the unresolvable dilemma of security/freedom as it is against a society whose rules have been made by men for men.

The same dilemma was faced by many Germans when the Nazis came into power. The Nazis offered order in place of chaos, employment in place of idleness, national pride in place of humiliation, clarity and certainty of direction over confusion of purpose and meaning. In short, they offered security in the face of disintegration and anarchy. But the price was freedom, and those who were unwilling to pay the price were simply destroyed.

The conflict between freedom and security is analogous to another conflict, the need to be distinct and the need to belong, the need to make up one's own mind about things and the need to yield to the pressures of the group. The fashion industry thrives on these two needs and on the willingness of the person à la mode to walk the razor's edge between the two.

Fairness under a socialist system is considered to be summed up in a slogan: from each according to his ability, to each according to his need. This might be parodied by the one who favors free enterprise as "to each according to his ability, from each according to his need."

Let not the reader think that we are simply concerned with verbal definitions. No martyr has gone to the stake or stood in front of a firing squad with a dictionary under his or her arm. The ambiguity of freedom is more profound than simply saying that on the one hand there is freedom *to* and on the other freedom *from*. Freedom is freedom and it is against the threat of loss of freedom, real or imagined, that men and women have fought, suffered, and died.

Voltaire said that all religious problems boil down to one question: should the shirt be worn inside or outside the trousers? If only it were so. If only the problem "monism" or "dualism" could be solved so easily. There always has been a faction that feels conflict comes from confused words and that could we but clarify our words, or get rid of words, or agree that others use different words, then all our differences and conflicts would drop away. Esperanto, a universal language, would usher in the millenium. But can conflict be so easily resolved? Are religious problems simply problems of semantics? If we stopped using words, even if we got rid of thought, would conflict thereby be eliminated?

There is a koan in the *Mumonkan* in which Zen master Shuzan held up a staff to the assembly of monks and said, "You monks, if you say this is a staff you are mistaken. If you say it is not a staff you lie. Now, what is it?"

Some say that Shuzan wanted to free his disciples from the snare of words, but is that all he wanted to do? Do the two faces in Figure 1 come into being because of words? The two Seis are not verbal formulations. To see Zen as a set of riddles showing the inadequacy of language and thought to come to terms with existence is to confuse the medicine with the cure. There is no doubt that words are inadequate, and Zen when practiced correctly shows this, but this is not all. When the sun rises it shows what a poor source of light a candle is. But this, in itself, is not all. When the sun rises, it rises!

The belief that conflict comes from words and thought was rife in Buddha's time too. Pundits of the day felt that could we but clarify words, or get rid of words, or agree that others use different words, then all differences and conflicts would simply drop away. Some of the pundits had a questionnaire made up of a "quadrilemma" with which they confronted and confounded the teachers of the day. The Buddha himself was confronted with the questionnaire on several occasions and each time simply rejected it. He said it was a *viewpoint* that was the problem.

"Is the Tathagata [Buddha] after death?"
"This is but a viewpoint, monk."
"Is the Tathagata not after death?"
"Both is he and is he not after death?"
"Neither is he nor is he not after death?"
"These are but viewpoints, monk."[5]

Mumon in his poem on this koan says:

The moon among the clouds is ever the same [one]:
Valleys and mountains are in constant change.
What a happy thing this is.
Is this one, is this two?[6]

If we try to surrender the moon, the light of our life will grow dim, meaning it will be lost and true hope destroyed forever. If we surrender the valleys and mountains, our life will be spent in a vacuous glow, empty of interest and challenge. Is it one, is it two?

4

The Mind of Ambiguity

*Every day Zen master Zuigan used to call to himself,
"O Master!" and would answer himself, "Yes?" "Be
awake, be awake!" he would exclaim and then answer, "Yes! Yes!" "Do not be deceived by others, any
day, any time." "No, I will not."[1]*

"The eye with which I see God is the eye with which
God sees me." This famous aphorism of Meister Eckhart
gives us a way into this koan. With one and the same eye
one both sees and is seen. With one and the same voice
Zuigan calls and answers: "Be awake, be awake!" "Yes!
Yes!" "Do not be deceived by others." "No, I will not."
Who is it that calls? Who answers? Who are the others
who deceive us?

Anyone who has traveled across the ocean by liner has
had the experience of being, as it were, *at the center* of
a vast plate. In a similar way, if one has gazed at the stars

when the sky is clear, one has had the impression of being under a great dome, again at the center. Each lives his or her life as though at the very center of impressions: sounds come from "out there," as do smells, tastes, and sights. All converge on me, me as the center of awareness, a center which is a point from which all is viewed. Not only through the senses does the world converge on me, but in time I am at the center from which radiates the past and the future; in imagination too I am at the center of all my fantasies. Furthermore, my values are biased in such a way that the death of thousands in China leaves me unmoved, of hundreds in a nearby province makes me concerned, of scores in the town in which I live leaves me dismayed, of several in my street hits me badly, while one death in my own household devastates me.

That this is universal is certain: all nations either secretly or overtly claim to be at the center, to be God's chosen ones; mythologies place the human being at the pinnacle; cosmologies place the earth at the center of the universe. In the British Isles maps of the world have Britain at the center, in North America it is the American continent which has this place.

But simultaneously with being the center, I am also at the periphery. While I stargaze, the awful sense of my own insignificance and transience can strike. The vastness of space and the uncountable numbers of stars force upon me a feeling of contingency and of being outside what really matters. In my own life my dependency upon others and upon the world is brought home to me daily, even hourly. My boss beckons and I go; the policeman raises his hand and I stop. I am tied to my fellow creatures with threads of uncertain strength. Without money, I am impotent; without language, dumb. The sense of being forsaken, alien, abandoned is the extreme sense of being at the periphery of where the action is, an outsider. This feeling is never so strong perhaps as when one is stranded without money in a country whose language one cannot speak.

The progress of science has also steadily displaced humankind from the center to the periphery. The earth, from being the fixed center of the universe, has become just a ball of matter whirling around a sun which roams around the galaxy. Human beings have fallen from the pinnacle of creation to find themselves but one kind of animal among myriads of others; the human mind has been dethroned and in its place we have a rabble of contending complexes.

However, it is not that I am now the center, now at the periphery, but *simultaneously* I am the center and at the periphery. This means that there is always present within me a certain tautness that constantly veers toward tension, tension which on occasions can become severe stress. Even looking at so innocent a thing as, say, a bookshelf has inextricably woven within it this tension that comes from being the center and at the periphery simultaneously. Rudolf Arnheim, a well-known art critic and author, says, "As I sit in my study my glance runs into the bookshelf and is blocked from further progress in that direction. The bookshelf responds to my approach by a counteraction: it advances towards me. But as my eyes rest upon it, I can also make it display the opposite tendency, namely that of yielding to my approach by moving away from me, thus joining the direction of my glance. Every visible object exhibits this twofold dynamic tendency in relation to the viewer's self: it approaches and recedes."[2]

Although we can experience now being the center and now being at the periphery, the *simultaneity* of being-at-the-center/being-at-the-periphery (see Fig. 2, p. 68) can only be known through direct intuition; an intuition that carries with it, because of the inherent

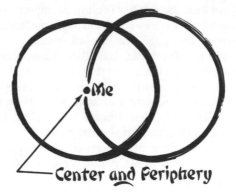

Figure 2

conflict, considerable hazard. We shall explore this
hazard more fully in a short while. For the moment let it
be said that we do not "experience" this simultaneity,
but only its consequences. Experience indeed is accumulated precisely in an attempt to nullify, or at least
mute, the conflict in this most fundamental viewpoint.

In Figure 2, there is one point that is simultaneously at
the center of the circle on the left and on the periphery
of the other. In the same way, me-as-center and
me-as-periphery are one viewpoint, which is me.[3]

Before going on, let us see first where this discussion
is taking us. In recent times it has become starkly
impressed upon our minds that we may well destroy the
world in a paroxysm of nuclear fury. This is not so much
frightening—the prospect is somehow too vast—as
unbelievable. When one sees the kind of destruction a
nuclear war can release portrayed on film or television,
one is anxious, but overriding the anxiety is the question
"Why?" "How can we even contemplate this?"

Some say that wars and fighting arise because of an
"aggressive instinct" or because people are naturally

aggressive. But what is this word "instinct" other than a veiled way of saying "I don't know." If people are naturally aggressive, how is it that millions are able to live together, interact, and support each other in large cities?

Others say that conflict comes from conflicting experience—a mother, for example, is both loving and hostile—or that it comes from a "conflict of desires," or from the famous Oedipus complex. But these beg the question, as "conflict" is implied in the answers given to why there is conflict. Conditioning is also a favored explanation. Human beings are antipathetic to others because they are conditioned into being antipathetic. But what about two male lions who fight? Are they conditioned? Conflict seems inherent in nature, both within species and between species.

Others say that conflict arises because of a loss of homeostasis and inner equilibrium. This again is much like saying that conflict arises because conflict arises. Others say more subtly that conflict is a way of maintaining equilibrium. Then, too, there is the explanation that conflict comes from the Fall. A sin was committed many eons ago of which we are the heirs.

The problem with these explanations is that the cause of conflict—and its attendant consequences of anxiety, guilt, anger, fighting, and so on—lies outside our responsibility and therefore beyond our control. The situation would therefore appear to be hopeless. If I am not responsible, then I must endure the situation as best I can. But what if, basically, I *am* responsible? What if the nature of man and woman (that is, me) is such that conflict is inevitable but that each of us is responsible for that nature by adopting a viewpoint? And, moreover, what if our nature is such that we cannot help adopting a viewpoint?

When Zuigan calls and is called, who is it that calls?

What is this One voice that beckons and answers? In the answer to this question lies the secret to conflict and to ecstasy. In this one call, one response, lies heaven and hell. Eckhart says the One eye sees and is seen. Another famous writer, Teilhard de Chardin, says, "The whole of life lies in the verb *seeing*. If not ultimately, at least essentially. . . . *To see or to perish* is the very condition laid upon everything that makes up the universe."[4] To see is not simply to see with the eyes; it is to see with the ears, nose, tongue, intellect, intuition. If Teilhard is right in his assertion, then the whole of life lies in being a viewpoint, and we should not look to the vagaries of, say, accident or evolution to understand the place of a viewpoint in the world. The viewpoint is the world. Nothing can live without seeing, and seeing (in all senses of the word) requires a viewpoint.

In the early seventies a most interesting book was written called *The Algiers Motel Incident*. Two black men had been shot in a Detroit motel by two white policemen. A reporter interviewed eight different eyewitnesses and wrote an account of what each reported. Eight different worlds emerged. One might be tempted to say, "But that is not eight different worlds, just eight different ways of interpreting the facts." The reporter, if I remember, gave what he felt "really" happened. But did he say what "really" happened? Suppose that there was some superior being who saw "all" that happened, saw it in fact through the eyes of the eight people, and reported upon this; can we say "this is what really happened," or ought we to say "this is yet another world, although more complex"? Distinction must be made between viewpoint and opinion: opinions, judgments, ideas, even outright lies and deliberate distortions are all lenses by which the view of the viewpoint is modified.

The word *view* is ambiguous and deliberately chosen

for its ambiguity. This can be clarified by asking what is meant when one asks for a room with a view. By view, does one mean a scene to be viewed or the opportunity to view it? Both are implied, but they are different from each other.

It is no accident that we *simultaneously* see and are seen. As an example to help show this, let us take a stage play. Arnheim, whom we have just quoted, says that there are two viewpoints which have to be taken into account by the director: the viewpoint *from* the stage and the viewpoint *of* the stage, in other words the viewpoint of the actors and the viewpoint of the audience. A director "moves back and forth between stage and audience, trying to organize the stage action according to its own logic and checking on what the projection offers from the slanted perspective of the audience." Each of us is a stage director, the one who calls and is called, the actor and the audience.

Inevitably we return to the question, the central theme of this book and of life: how can there be two? This is the fundamental ambiguity. Zuigan says, "Do not be deceived by others." What kind of deception is this? What others do or what others are? Could he mean, in other words, that others are an illusion? If so, is the one who is deceived not also an illusion? This would be—indeed often is—one way by which the apparent conflict could be resolved between the immutable, indivisible One and the evident, indisputable two. The one voice alone is real. But then who is it that calls, who is it that hears? Is not the immutable One also an illusion? But even an illusion is viewed, and realizing this we return inexorably again to the viewpoint, the same viewpoint from which arise this question and all questions, this dream and all dreams.

The Other is that which to me is both central and peripheral; it too shares in the ambiguity, as we have seen. Later we shall point up how all life can be looked upon as an unending pilgrimage in search of an unambiguous Other. However, although the Other is a constant, what is seen as the Other changes ceaselessly. As long as I am awake, I am always seeing something; this something is the Other in the guise of people, buildings, cars, thoughts, feelings, dreams, illusions; the Other can even simply be a presence. All are the Other in disguise, all are the appearances of the Other. R.D. Laing, a well-known psychiatrist and writer, wrote of what he felt was the potentially tragic paradox of our life, that "our relatedness to others is an essential aspect of our being, as is our separateness, but any particular person is not a necessary part of our being."[5]

This, in a more general way, is what is being said here. With the viewpoint comes the Other (with the view comes the view); if we see, there must be something "out there" to be seen. The Other is as essential to life as the view. But no particular Other is essential, no particular center (to which to be peripheral) is a necessary part of our being. Yet our deepest need is for some particular and necessary center which will relieve us of the burden of ambiguity with its attendant conflicts. Where is that center? It is this search that gives life the quality of an unending journey. The Wandering Jew, the Flying Dutchman, Moby Dick, Ulysses, Gilgamesh, the quest for the Holy Grail, the Promised Land, Shangri-La, Joshu's asking "What is the Way?"—all are evidence of this search for the unknown center.

Religion, art, philosophy, science are the great vehicles used in the search; a search which from its very nature is doomed to fail. Nevertheless the search by its nature must be conducted to resolve the untenable conflict in me-as-center/me-as-periphery. We search for the center, while being the center, "like one in water crying, 'I thirst.'"

The more intensely the search is conducted, the more clearly it is recognized that the only adequate center, the one that can finally put an end to this restlessness, is me-as-center. But this simply heightens the conflict because the more intensely me-as-center is established, the more intensely is established me-as-periphery, its complement, and so the search for an end to the conflict is increased and the search for the Holy Grail intensified. The hunger for the view is intensified with the view. This sets up a vicious circle, like the feedback from a loudspeaker into a microphone and back out through the loudspeaker. As the volume increases in intensity to an unbearable degree, so the conflict too increases unbearably.

Let us sum up. "Me" is the concrete eye of experience and is single, it is One. This eye, however, looks and is looked at simultaneously.[6] Alternatively, this could be expressed by saying that it looks "inward" and "outward" at one and the same time. Each of the two has equal claim on the other, because each arises because of the other. I see something, say, an apple, because it is there to be seen. But the apple is only one of many things that I see, and of these many things (including the apple) I am the center. However, it is not only I who see the apple; there are many who see it. For the many who see it (including me), the apple is the center. Thus the viewpoint "me" is the center and periphery simultaneously, but although each arises because of the other, they are mutually exclusive. It is like two cocks fighting: each sees itself as the One and cannot coexist with the other. But whereas one cock can prevail, because one cock can be stronger than the other, there can be no such resolution where each of the protagonists is equal to the other through mutual dependency. This fundamental viewpoint is nevertheless One and an unresolved contradiction would irrevocably destroy the

One. Thus, although on the one hand there can be no resolution, on the other there has to be a resolution, not sometime in the future, but at the very instant the contradiction arises.

The resolution, we would suggest, is what we call *life*. Life is both the viewpoint as experience, and the dynamism inherent in the conflict as action. To quote Teilhard again: "Man, the center of perspective, is at the same time the *center of construction* of the universe." Later he says that man is "a *whole* which unfolds."[7] I would like to go further and say that all living beings are, each in their own way, *the* center of perspective (or a viewpoint) and at the same time *the* center of construction of the universe. Each is a Oneness that unfolds. In the words of Hakuin, "From the beginning all beings are Buddha." Not a beginning in time, but a beginning that is always now.

This "oneness that unfolds" unfolds as experience and growth, as culture and evolution. We must see in this a knot: the Gordian knot of antiquity,[8] the endless knot of the Tibetans. Not only is there ambiguity then—"me-as-center/me-as-periphery—there is also the ambiguity "one/two." There is Zuigan and the other; there is Zuigan and the one call. Is there a unity beyond the ambiguity, or not? If there is, how does the ambiguity arise? If there is not, why do we struggle so hard to find the unity beyond ambivalence? Putting this succinctly, ambiguity has two faces, but one face of the ambiguity reveals there is no ambiguity: only Oneness, but a Oneness that itself is not unambiguous.[9]

When something is seen, it becomes a center in its own right, and a tension is set up between me-as-center/me-as-periphery. We illustrated this with the example given by Rudolf Arnheim of looking at a bookshelf. Let us be clear that by a center we do not simply mean the middle or geometrical center, but, as Arnheim would call it, a dynamic center, "a center of a field of forces, a focus from which forces issue and toward which forces converge."[10] He goes on to say, "Speaking generally, one can assert that every visual field comprises a number of centers, each of which tries to draw the others into subservience . . . The overall balance of all these competing aspirations determines the structure of the whole and that whole is organized around what I call the balancing center."[11]

When I look at the bookshelf, there is then a competition: who is to be the center? With an object this does not present too much of a problem to most people as one can alternate at will—now taking, now yielding the center; now being the center, now the periphery—and the situation is under control. This can be verified by anyone. Just select at random something as the center and you will find that everything immediately arranges itself around this center. Then simply be the center yourself. Everything is rearranged accordingly. In the first case it is almost as though you are "outside" looking in, in the second as though you are "inside" looking out.

We said that it was not a problem to most people, but to some it is an excruciating problem. One mental patient said, "Things began to take on life, to exist. The stone jug decorated with blue flowers was there facing me, defying me with its presence, with its existence. To conquer my fear I looked away. My eyes met a chair, then a table, *they were alive, asserting their presence*" (emphasis added).[12] They were alive, asserting their presence—they were in effect "looking back." Instead of there being an alternation of now center, now periphery, there is a locking, one is both center and periphery simultaneously and *in full awareness of the fact.* The barrier of experience which has been patiently built up to protect is broken through. It is like two mirrors face to face, but each mirror wishing to dominate, to be *the*

center. The following is from the author's own experience:

> I was suffering from insomnia and had hardly slept for
> a week. I went to the bathroom and while there hap-
> pened to catch sight of myself in the mirror. I looked
> at the reflection of my eyes intently for a moment,
> caught the eyes looking back in a kind of horror. The
> horror reflected in the eyes and so created more hor-
> ror. Suddenly I found myself caught in a vortex of hor-
> ror which augments.

It is not the surrogate Other that generates the horror,
but the *fact* of the Other. The horror is awakened
entirely by the ambiguity of 'me,' me-as-*center*/me-as-*periphery*. In that the self is manifestly one, this ambiguity
is a wound in the very heart of hearts—a wound that is
the threat of being devoured: me-as-*center* threatened by
me-as-*periphery,* and me-as-*periphery* threatened by
me-as-*center.* The threat is therefore of endless but total
annihilation, an engulfment without bottom: hell itself in
its most terrible aspect. This devouring potential of the
self by the self has been symbolized by the ancients as
the uroborus, a snake swallowing its own tail.

How difficult it is to look into the eyes of another, how
uncomfortable it can make us feel to hold the gaze of
another, even for a short while. Why is this? After a few
seconds at most, a tension arises, then a feeling of
irritation at the other for holding one's gaze, then
hostility, and, if the encounter continues and the
situation does not turn into some kind of game, or the
other is not converted into an object, we become
aggressive.

The author was attacked in the street by a stranger
whose gaze he had held for just too long. It turned out
that the man was addicted to some very harsh drugs and

Figure 3.

no doubt the explosives in the attack were furnished by them. But the trigger that set the explosion off, also without doubt, was the prolonged eye contact. Visitors to New York City are advised to avoid eye contact, and part of the nightmarish quality that this city has for some comes from this studious avoidance of eye contact.

Animals, too, experience hostility in a gaze. Why else would staring eyes be used as a form of camouflage? The Mexican bull's-eye moth, for example, has a spot on either wing that gives the appearance of malevolent eyes. There is a species of caterpillar that has a false head which, in times of danger, is inflated and on either side of this head is a large false eye. Another species of caterpillar has two eyes on one side and when it is disturbed it curls up into a ball giving the appearance of a face with, once again, the malevolent eyes.

The hostility in the gaze is twofold. In the first place it releases the threat of the malignant wound being opened. At the same time the other, in defending himself from this very same threat, simply confirms the threat, and so a vicious circle is established.

The ambiguous viewpoint is therefore not simply a benign quirk. On the contrary, it is a malignant wound that threatens constantly to annihilate the very basis of our being. The simultaneous recognition of two centers cannot endure: one center must give way, or be forced to give way. Good manners, for example, decree that one does not stare at others because to do so is "rude." Instead one holds the gaze of the other for a moment and then looks away. Protocol is another method of handling this situation. The higher in the hierarchy, the nearer the center, and when two people meet, the one lower in the hierarchy keeps the eyes respectfully lowered or looking straight ahead. A further twist was once given in that people in the presence of a king would not turn their backs on the sovereign, but retire backward, bowing with eyes lowered. Since the subjects face him, the king is acknowledged as the single center; he is reciprocally raised relative to the one bowing, and the acknowledgment of his being center is reinforced.

There are a thousand subtle variations possible in the granting or appropriating of the center.[13] In office politics, who goes to whose office for a meeting determines who is not and who is the center. A manager that comes from behind his desk to meet with a visitor yields his position of being center. *Who* sits *where* relative to the head of an oblong table, *who* sits next to *whom*, whose office is on the top floor, next to the president, and so on—all of these are ways of coping with the question "Am I the center to which others turn, or is another the center to which I turn?" A mark of respect once was to circumambulate around a person or sacred spot—an obvious way to grant that the other is the center.

Another way of handling the situation is to objectify,

or indeed to petrify (meaning to turn the other or oneself to stone). Stereotyping, denying others the right of individuality, is one example of this. How can a member of an amorphous mass—a Limey, a Yank, a Jew—be the center? It was precisely this mechanism of stereotyping and turning living beings into objects that made it possible for the scourge of the Holocaust to ride rampant across Europe. But, of course, not only did Germans reduce Jews to objects, but white men do it to black men, men to women, managers to workers, and vice versa. An object is simply a passive center like the bookcase and can create no opposition or threat.

Modern man tends to smile condescendingly at "primitive" people who, it is said, "animate" the world around them, creating tree spirits, spirits in the wind, and spirits in the mountains; and having fairies, elves, demons, and gods , making all nature alive. But is it the primitive who animates the world or the modern man who "objectifies" it, that is, makes the world into an object? Is not one of the horrifying aspects of our society its tendency to objectify things? Cattle, for example, each of which once had a name, are now simply "Big Macs" on legs waiting for the hamburger roll. Chickens are machines for laying eggs. The idea that trees and plants are responsive causes a titter. With the help of the Behaviorists and the computer, we are steadily reducing human beings to objects identified by numbers. This objectifying is but a way of protecting ourselves against the horror of being looked at while looking, the horror of sinking into the vortex of center/periphery/center/periphery.

However, the reciprocity of me-as-center/me-as-periphery means that if I turn the Other into an object, then I turn myself into an object at the same time. In fact some people turn themselves into completely immobile objects and can stay this way for years, having to be fed

and cared for in an institution. It is called a catatonic
state.

To be an object means that one is no longer
responsible. At one level this means that one is no longer
a source of initiative and decisions. It is not, therefore,
in the least surprising that Hess, the commandant of
Auschwitz concentration camp, denied responsibility
for the death of the Auschwitz Jews. The S.S. man was a
uniform, an armband, a Nazi salute. It could be said that,
in a way, Hess was right. He was not responsible for the
massacre of the Jews. His responsibility was for turning
himself into an object; this sets up its own kind of vortex:
the more harm I do to others, the more I deny
responsibility, and therefore the more harm I will do to
others.

It might well be asked why it was said that the
intuition of me-as-center/me-as-periphery carries with it
considerable hazard. How could it be said that this
intuition gives the key to heaven and hell, to the ultimate
in ecstasy and to the depths of horror? On the face of it
this would seem an exaggeration. But it is nevertheless
contended that it is so, that not only is this intuition the
key to the understanding of suffering, anxiety, frustration, and confusion, but it is also the key to understanding conflict: why people fight, why animals fight, why
there are wars, the reason for man's inhumanity to man.
Not only this, it is also and at the same time a key to
understanding—love, both romantic and divine, and it is
the key to understanding profound religious experience.
Let us now consider this further.

5
The Center as Other

Ejaku (a well-known monk of his day) asked Enen,
"What is your name?" Enen, an equally famous
monk, said, "Ejaku." Ejaku said, "My name is Ejaku."
Enen said, "Then my name is Enen." Ejaku roared
with laughter.[1]

The injunction "love thy neighbor as thyself" is not,
strictly speaking, a moral or ethical imperative, but
rather it is simply the reasonable thing to do. My
neighbor *is* myself. The other *is* me as the Other,
me-as-periphery. It is the failure to appreciate the
ambiguity of "me"—me-as-center/me-as-periphery—that
makes this fundamental truth difficult to see. It is like the
inside and the outside of a cup: the inside is the cup,
the outside is the cup. But that does not say the inside is
the same as the outside, nor that the inside and outside
are different cups.

We cannot say that me-as-center or me-as-periphery is "within a person" or that they are "subjective." Furthermore, once we intuitively see into the truth of the oneness of all people—indeed of all life—all are necessary. I cannot be me without you. You relieve me of the burden of being you. Your success relieves me of the need for succeeding as you have succeeded.

The vital relation between I and Thou is the working out of the ambiguity of life; or putting this differently, one could say that ambiguity is another word for life. The constant, the static, or the certain are simply aspects of the ambiguous. A well-known English physicist says much the same thing:

> I think people get it upside down when they say the unambiguous is the reality and the ambiguous merely uncertainty about what is really unambiguous. Let's turn it around the other way: the ambiguous is the reality and the unambiguous is merely a special case of it, where we finally manage to pin down some very special aspect.[2]

But still the problem remains: if you are me in the guise of being you, and if I am you in the guise of being me, why did Buddha say, "Throughout heaven and earth *I alone* am the honored One"? If Christ and the Father are One, which is the One—the Father or Christ? You and I are separated: which is the true me?

There is a longing in each for some final consummation, some "end of the road." If I yield to you as center, does that mean that I am not center? Try as I may—and there are many ways of trying—I cannot let go of the truth of me-as-center. It is not an experience, it is there. Everything comes toward me: this object is near, that far; this one is on this side, that on the other side. Time also stretches before and after, passing this point here and now where I am. How can it be said I am not center? But I look into your eyes and see the same perplexity and the same conclusion. So I brace against you while the question flashes through my mind again. If you have more power, I will lower my eyes; if I am less certain than you, I might look away. At the beginning of the fight when touching gloves, boxers stare at each other, both prompting and seeking the telltale signs of weakness and strength. Sometimes the fight is decided in those few moments. Some Sumo wrestlers, it is said, will put their opponents out of the ring by looking at them.

The yearning for oneness becomes a claim and the claim can erupt into war to destroy the other. Wars, even the war that could destroy earth, have this same mechanism. Peace demonstrations, United Nations conferences, disarmament treaties, these will not do away with war because we have war in our heart of hearts. They may modify the kind of war that is waged and to this end are worthwhile, but while I have the worm in my heart, I need not seek for whom the siren wails: it wails for me.

On the face of it, this is pure pessimism. Is mankind therefore doomed by an ambiguity over which he has no control? Yes. Doomed, but also exalted. It is because of this same ambiguity that mankind has the capacity to love, to experience the divine and to awaken, which is to come to a pinnacle indescribable but nevertheless real. But let us take things in order. First we will talk of love: profane love, then divine love. Then we will explore some fundamental religious experiences of mankind and show they can be understood as an outcome of the one/two ambiguity.

It has been said, *"L'enfer, c'est les autres."* "Hell is other people." Sometimes we feel that if it were not for other people, everything would be all right. But if this is the case, why is it that solitary confinement is such an extreme form of punishment? Why is it that people love to talk with each other? Why is it that people flock to cities to live with others? Why is it that people dread ostracism and rejection? And how is it that although eyes are used in movies to awaken horror in the audience (the sudden switch to the unblinking eyes of a cat or a doll, of a blind man or corpse), lovers are able, indeed long, to look into the eyes of the beloved?

> Her glances first came hesitant and sidelong
> Then soft and shy with love
> A while they rested on me motionless
> Then slowly turned away.
> Her pupils widening behind long lashes
> Told of the admiration she felt.[3]

In place of resisting the other and sealing the other off with hate, there is now a yearning and love. The inevitability, the rightness, and instantaneous but eternal quality of "falling in love" comes when the surrogate seems to become for a moment the Other, the wall becomes a window, and there is a feeling of purity and peace.

Romantic love has always been a never-ending source of fascination for human beings. The same theme of boy meets girl, falls in love, meets obstacles, and finally overcomes them is repeated endlessly in myths, stories, plays, films, and soap operas. What is this fascination? Is romantic love simply the byproduct of the sex "instinct," some accidental decoration in life; or is it something else?

> I don't know how to love him
> What to do, how to move him.[4]

A girl sings of her love for a man. The man is Christ, the girl is Mary Magdalene, and the song is from a rock opera, *Jesus Christ Superstar.* Is this simply a case of profanity? Is there not a radical difference between a girl going glassy-eyed over some superstar and the love of Mary Magdalene for Christ? Or has the song writer stumbled across or discovered the fundamental truth: that samsara is nirvana: that everyday mind is the way: that the profane is the sacred in disguise.

St. John of the Cross, a Christian mystic of the sixteenth century, wrote poetry. One of the most inspired is called "Between the Soul and the Bridegroom." It is said that he wrote this after hearing a girl pass by his window singing a love song. Was it something like a song that Frank Sinatra used to sing:

> Where are you, where are you keeping
> Now that I want you so badly I could cry?

St. John's poem begins:

> Where have you hidden away
> Beloved, and left me here to mourn?
> Having wounded me you fled
> Like the hart I followed on
> Behind you, crying out, calling—
> But you were gone.[5]

The words are similar, but what about the inspiration?

What is the difference between profane love and sacred love? The first yearns for the body of the beloved, the second for the soul? But is this the case? Do either really know what they are yearning for? Can they know? In love, be it profane or divine, there is a unity, a oneness, a coming together. But a coming together of what? Joe and Mary? The soul and God? Or the self with the self as the Self?

The look between lovers is the very wellspring of romantic love. What can the look tell us about religious love? Can this encounter of the look and the looked at, and the unresolvable ambiguity of who is looking and whom looked at, give a key to open some of the mysteries of divine love?

On the one hand we have the romantic encounter with the eyes of the beloved:

> Drink to me only with thine eyes
> And I will pledge with mine.[6]

On the other we have a refrain in praise of Krishna:

> From the moment our eyes first me
> Our longing grew.
> He was not only the desirer,
> I not only the desired.[7]

Again let us ask: if the look can be the source of horror and hostility, how is it now the source of love?

With a fixed stare a contest is started. The more alike the contestants, the more rapidly the contest will turn to aggression. But what if the eyes are yielding? Instead of hard, staring eyes, they are laughing and soft. Who is the center? Is she claiming the center or yielding the center? It is no longer a contest of me-as-*center* and me-as-*periphery,* but a coming together of *me*-as-center and *me*-as-periphery. The blessed wound is healed. Each "me" is affirmed in a vortex of affirmation leading to an ecstasy of One Self.

The encounter with the other through the look is neither trivial nor mundane.

> But for me the climax was that direct glance from the
> eyes of the saint-like, white-robed figure on his crim-
> son throne. It seemed as though the center of my very
> being was riven, my soul transported by a rapturous
> ecstasy of emotion to a pinnacle of feeling such as I
> had not known a human being could experience and
> survive.[8]

This is not a girl speaking about her encounter with her
beloved, but the description of an encounter between
the eyes of a monk and the eyes of the Pope. But did the
monk really encounter the Pope? If so, why does not
everyone experience such ecstasy when the Pope looks
at them?

The look is two, ambiguous, looking and looked at.
And the look is one. It is timeless. The other as a person,
a Pope, or a beautiful woman is a trigger that releases this
vortex of affirmation of me by me, of me the self
affirming the self as me.

Suppose Freud had it all topsy-turvy? Suppose the Id
is really Oneness. What if the fear of death is not the fear
of castration, but the other way around? What if sex is
really a sublimation of religion, and conscience not a
surrogate father but a source from which a father gets his
authority?

Does the reader feel that there is a "nothing but"
denigration of religion and God at work? On the
contrary, it means that even the raising of a hand to bid
good-day is a mystical encounter. Religion is not
subjective: the soul is not *in* the body, heaven is not *in*
the sky. It is impossible to talk this way: in, out, space,
time. These are but filters to hold apart the inseparable.
They are ways to put the basic ambiguity into a cage. In
this way we can live in relative peace, with anxiety but
no horror, with contentment but no ecstasy.

For some, either because the bars are rusted or the beast too vigorous, the cage is not strong enough and they are filled with a restlessness, a divine discontent, and they have to look down the throat of the monster, and the religious quest is born. But are all religious quests the same?

I would suggest they are not. Suppose that there are two paths, leading in complementary but opposite directions: one with the emphasis on looking, the other with the emphasis on being looked at; one toward *me*-as-center, the other toward *me*-as-periphery. The key point about me-as-center/me-as-periphery must be borne in mind here; we can never have one without the other; this is why it is only a question of *emphasis*. Both paths lead toward *me*, or the Self, but from opposite directions. The first the Japanese would call the way of Self power; the second, the way of Other power; in India the first has been called Jnana; the second, Bhakti. In Hinduism there are the two paths of Jnana and Bhakti, and in Christianity there are also the two paths. And of course again it is only a question of emphasis, for there is always an element of Bhakti in Jnana, and vice versa.

In terms of religious experience, the Bhakti path, or the way of divine love, leads to *enlightenment,* and the Jnana path, or the way of knowing, leads to samadhi. The word enlightenment has been used somewhat indiscriminately in the West, which has tended to obscure differences important to perceive—the difference between samadhi and enlightenment, and the difference between these two and awakening.

The way of the Christian mystic, the way of divine love, is toward an encounter with the Other: a union as an act of love. It is a way along which it is assumed that God and man are of fundamentally different essence. Unity is achieved through the grace of God. It is by His grace that the unbridgeable is bridged, and it was in the birth, life, and death of Christ that this bridge was made known to man. Enlightenment takes the form of an encounter, and this encounter is the encounter with a presence which is interpreted as the presence of God, or Christ, or the divine, but which is also oneself at the same time. "The Father and I are One."

This encounter with the divine presence is often seen as an intense light:

> The disciples had not seen Jesus because of the great light in which he was, or which was about him; for their eyes were darkened because of the great light in which he was. But they saw only the light, which shot forth many light rays. And the light rays were not like one another, but the light was of diverse kinds, and it was of diverse types, from below upwards, one ray more excellent than the other . . . in one immeasurable glory of light; it stretched from under the earth right up to heaven.[9]

In the Hindu tradition, this encounter with light appears in the account of Arjuna's meeting with Krishna, who appeared "glowing everywhere as a mass of light, hard to discern (dazzling) on all sides with the radiance of the flaming fire and the sun."[10]

And in the Sufi tradition:

> Thou who are clothed in the most beautiful of divine lights, may thou manifest Thyself to me in the most beautiful of epiphanies, show me the light of Thy most dazzling face.[11]

Sufi, Christian, and Hindu literature are suffused in this dazzling light and it is not surprising that this encounter should be called *enlightenment*. It can be understood as the whirl of me-as-center/me-as-periphery, or if one prefers, as an oscillation of now one, now the other, in which each encounters the other and the encounter itself is oneness. The mutual affirmation of the self as other and the other as self.

This encounter, or enlightenment, is not simply the province of mystics or monks, but can come to people from out of the blue:

> Rapt in Beethoven's music, I closed my eyes and watched a silver glow which shaped itself into a circle with a central focus brighter than the rest. The circle became a tunnel of light proceeding from some distant sun in the heart of the Self. Swiftly and smoothly I was borne through the tunnel and as I went the light turned from silver to gold. There was an impression of drawing strength from a limitless sea of power and a sense of deepening peace. The light grew brighter but was never dazzling or alarming. I came to a point where time and motion ceased. In my recollection it took the shape of a flat-topped rock, surrounded by a summer sea, with a sandy pool at its foot. The dream scene vanished and I am absorbed in the Light of the Universe, in Reality glowing like fire with the knowledge of itself, without ceasing to be one and myself, merged like a drop of quicksilver in the Whole, yet still separate as a grain of sand in the desert. The peace that passes all understanding and the pulsating energy of creation are one in the center in the midst of conditions where all opposites are reconciled.[12]

This is a fairly contemporary encounter with the Other in an ecstasy of light, brilliant but never painful. "I am absorbed in the light of the universe . . . without ceasing to be one and myself." Is that one, is that two? There is a merging while remaining separate, peace but pulsation. This encounter shows clearly the ambiguity:

the light as center: "a silver glow which became a circle with a center, a distant sun"; the me-as-center: "I came to a point where time and motion ceased, a flat-topped rock surrounded by sea"; then an oscillation of me-as-center/me-as-periphery: "I am the light, without ceasing to be myself . . . merged, yet separate . . . peace and pulsating energy."

The following encounter is interesting because of the circumstances leading to it. The experience came not from a moment of exaltation, but from a moment of rage, in which me-as-center was resisting me-as-periphery, reconciled by Oneness or Love:

> I was angry at the sarcasm and insensitivity people were showing toward things I felt strongly identified with. Suddenly, the anger dissolved into a vast love and it felt as though I were being drawn upward and out of the top of my head. At the same time a vast, brilliant, but not blinding light appeared. It seemed to be alive, or perhaps better, a living light, made up of infinite colors and yet white. It had a liquid quality and I felt intense love, joy, and peace, and wondered O why, O why have I waited so long.[13]

Enlightenment is the fruit of divine love; of yielding, even though momentarily, to the unknown center, present but not specific. But with the way of Knowing there is no *encounter* with the Other, but instead a merging in samadhi.

The word *samadhi* has for its roots *sam* and *adhi*. *Sam* means to combine, to mix or mingle. *Adhi* is somewhat more difficult to translate in that it means a pledge toward or a commitment; it also means conception (as when a woman conceives). It is an active term, whereas *sam* is a more reconciling term. *Sam* is an aspect of me-as-center and *adhi* is an aspect of me-as-periphery. Samadhi may be looked upon as a passive/active condition.

"How vast is the heaven of boundless samadhi!" There is no exalted state of the loving encounter with the Other; there is not the brilliance of the sun, but instead the serenity of the moon.

"How bright and transparent the moonlight of wisdom." There is a coolness in the place of the heat of enlightenment. However, it is still an intensely active state, as the word samadhi implies. There is a light, a diffuse light, just as when the moon is full overhead, and therefore just out of sight. There is also vast darkness. The sun of enlightenment also shines out of darkness, but this darkness is a kind of opaqueness. With samadhi the darkness is transparent, vast, unobstructed. In enlightenment it is as though two centers joined in an ecstatic dance without movement. In samadhi it is as though two peripheries merge, something like the "figure" and "ground" both being simultaneously ground.

> I was listening to music by Palestrina. The music came in wave upon wave and suddenly I was the music, my body was the music. The "feeling" lasted about four or five seconds and then it was as though something broke and the music and I were again separated.[14]

> When I reached this state it was like the moon in the water—transparent and penetrating. Impossible to disperse or obliterate, by rolling surges it was inspiring, alive, vivid all the time.[15]

Samadhi is not a placid or flaccid state. It is one of perfect balance and so without violence or tension, but it is dynamic and alive. It has a feeling of immense relief, not deadness or torpidity.

> Suddenly I stood still, filled with the realization that I
> had no body or mind. All I could see was one great illu-
> minating whole—omnipresent, perfect, lucid, serene.
> It was like an all-embracing mirror from which the
> mountains were projected as reflections.[16]

An all-embracing mirror, the mirror of samadhi. The
metaphor appears again and again in Zen: "a merging
with what is as one would merge with a surface."

What are we to make of this: on the one hand the
gentleness of moonlight, on the other hand the strength
of the sun? Does this not show that there are two
independent experiences of oneness, quite different,
indeed opposite? One a merging with what is, as one
would merge with a surface, and the other an encounter,
a going into. The one a Oneness, the other a falling away
of twoness. One samadhi, the other enlightenment. We
cannot rate them higher or lower than each other: they
are both significant and those who come to them have
the center of their lives touched. But neither samadhi
nor enlightenment is what is meant by *awakening*. The
following are accounts of true Zen awakening:

> The attendants poured hot water according to the
> rule. It splashed on my hand. The teacup fell to the
> ground and broke to bits with a loud noise. Suddenly
> the roots of doubt were cut. In my whole life I had
> never felt such joy. It was like waking from a dream.[17]

> Just as I was going to sit down, something broke
> abruptly before my face as if the ground were sinking
> away. I wanted to tell how I felt, but I could not ex-
> press it. Nothing in this world can be used as a simile
> to describe it. Immediately I went to find Hsiu. As
> soon as he saw me he said, "Congratulations! Congrat-
> ulations!"[18]

He [Kapleau-roshi] asked me some questions about
Mu. I thought about the first question he asked and
felt it didn't make any sense. He tried again and asked
another question. And again the only answer I could
give was an intellectual one. He tried a third question
and I felt a restlessness stir in me. I stood up and
walked away from him. The question suddenly went
deep and an eruption, a volcano, roared up from hara.
I shouted, "This is Mu! Mu! Mu!" I was yelling and
laughing.[19]

The next example tells of a young woman who
evidently had no Zen training, yet who nevertheless
encountered a true awakening flash. She had been told
by a specialist that she had less than two years to live,
and in a state of despair and rebellion she was walking in
the fields. She came to a water trough which was frozen
and some lambs were standing around. She broke the ice
for them and as she did so, she heard a voice within say,
"Having nothing, yet possessing all things." She looked
around, but found that she was quite alone. Suddenly, in
a flash, the grief, the bitterness, the sense of frustration
disappeared; all desire to possess power and glory for
herself vanished away and never came back. She later
associated her awakening with the words of a writer,
Bernard Bosanquet: "And now we are saved absolutely,
we need not say from what, we are at home in the
universe, and, in principle and in the main, feeble and
timid creatures as we are, there is nothing within the
world or without it that can make us afraid."[20]

Samadhi and enlightenment are describable—something happens. They last for some time, although this
time is not the time of the clock: there is an element of
eternity about them, time seems to slow down. Someone
called it the timeless moment; but it could also be called
the timeful moment. With awakening it is like a flash of

lightning;[21] anything that happens, happens before or after awakening. There is sometimes a light with awakening, but it is the light that comes after an explosion. When the light comes, "it" has already happened. For many there is no light. For some it is like a subterranean explosion; some would not even use the word explosion at all, but nevertheless there is that instantaneous cognitive quality. But whereas before there was something, now there is nothing. It has all the strangeness of walking through a building that has had the roof blown off. What before was enclosed is now open. It is like walking through walls, through and through without obstruction.

The Tibetan Book of the Dead says, "These two, mind whose nature is emptiness without any substance whatever, and mind which is vibrant and luminous, are inseparable; this is the truth-body of Buddha."[22] Awakening is to see into this truth-body.

Samadhi and enlightenment, this is the truth-body of Buddha. Enlightenment: the encounter and mutual adoration of two centers; samadhi: the merging of periphery with periphery, each center giving way, absorbed in the other. And Awakening? It is seeing into this truth-body. What does that mean? There are two: center and periphery. There are two: enlightenment and samadhi. Why the third? Is there something we have missed.

Enen calls Ejaku. These are two. Where is the third?

6

The Center as Mediator

Gettan said to a monk, "Keichu made a hundred carts. If you took off the wheels and removed the axle, then what would it be?"[1]

Zen master Mumon wrote a verse to the above koan:

> When a wheel spins rapidly
> Even a master wheelwright can't make head or tail of it. It moves in all directions in heaven and earth.
> North, south, east, and west.

In the *Tao-te-ching* it is written:

> Thirty spokes will converge
> In the hub of a wheel.
> But the use of the cart
> Will depend on the part
> Of the hub that is void.[2]

What good is a wheel that has no hub? What good is a life that has no meaning?

The word "I" is a strange one, perhaps the strangest of all. "I" has such a familiar and intimate ring, and yet what is "I"? On the one hand "I" seems so intimate, and on the other "I" is always eluding me. "I" in Latin is "ego" and ego has come to have a perjorative meaning. He has a big ego, we say. *I* don't agree. *I* don't think so. *I* want, I, I . . . . When Buddha said, "Throughout heaven and earth, I alone am the Honored One," did he mean *I* alone am the Honored One? Did Christ mean I and the Father are One? It is said that when Moses confronted God and asked how he should reply to the Israelites who asked for God's name, God said, "I am that I am." Gurdjieff, the great Russian spiritual teacher, wrote a book called *Life Is Real Only Then When I Am*. Why is "*I* am" wrong and "I am" right?

We would suggest that that which is generally thought of as ego is made up of three elements. uniqueness,[3] the center, and the word. In this triad none can be said to predominate. If it were not for the word, the center would never be fixed and therefore would not pose a problem. If it were not for uniqueness, the center would not be exclusive and therefore would not be offensive. If there were no center, none of this would arise.

We will explore first the elements of uniqueness and the center and, in the following chapter, the elements of the word.

It is said of Hitler: "He considered himself the universe's unique sentient center, the sole incarnate will it contained or had ever contained. 'I am, none else beside me.'" Is it possible that each of us sees ourself as the universe's unique sentient center? Not unique as a reward or a right, nor as a discovery or even an attainment, but as a given; or rather, as *the* given: "given that I am unique."

Are you unique?[4] Usually there is a kind of tension that arises when such a question is asked, an embarrassment or even irritation. Why is this? It is because if one is unique it cannot be questioned, for if it is questioned, how can one be unique? Humiliation and psychological pain have their roots in uniqueness being questioned; even affirming uniqueness is a denial of it. Uniqueness is incomparable, and to affirm it would be to display it for inspection, which in effect makes it "something" among other things. What joy it is to have uniqueness recognized without one's having to earn it! Is this not what all flatterers and confidence tricksters play upon?

It is all right to hint at one's uniqueness, or to display it obliquely, even to affirm it by denying; but not to step forward and say, "I am unique." When someone's hints are too blatant we feel embarrassed for that person, we laugh, turn away, are not quite sure what to say. We avoid such a person and say he or she is too egoistic, or has a "big" ego. But can we have too much, or even more or less, of something so absolute as uniqueness?

Uniqueness is so fundamental that it is scarcely capable of being comprehended. I am unique because "throughout heaven and earth I alone am the Honored One." But when I *insist* on this uniqueness. . . . When Gutei raises his finger, it is One. And when the assistant raises his? Ramana Maharishi says, "When it goes in, it is the Self; when it goes out, it is the self." But even this is too much. Even using I and *I* is too much. A tenth of an inch is all the difference between heaven and earth. Not even a tenth. "If you remove the axle, what would it be then?" How do you remove the hub and still have a wheel?

To *say* the universe is One is to divide it irrevocably. "Even raising a finger can split the universe in two."[5] Logically and existentially it is either one or two, or both, or neither. To say "because it is one it is two" makes no sense, which is why logically and existentially we can never come to terms with this mystery. It is also why, using logic and experience, we tread the six worlds of existence, flourishing and declining to flourish and decline again. Inextricably bound by the Gordian knot of ambiguity, our Janus like view of the world spins the tangled web of experience.

If we are One with the All, how can we possibly be lonely, how can we fail, where can death find a way in? If one, why two? But because at the very source of experience there *is* two, we have to rediscover Oneness or suffer unbearable pain. We rediscover Oneness as I am, as uniqueness through the center. *I* am is an assertion and affirmation, but that very assertion is a separation, a new wound. We attempt the impossible in asserting *I* am and so die constantly the death of separation. And as we are drawn down into this vortex of confusion, we grab out for love or religion, temporarily resisting the plunge to annihilation. But love is fickle and religion difficult and demanding. The way gets tougher, the knot strangles.

Nature has its own way of resolving "one but two." As the pendulum swings from the center outward and back again, is there one continuous swing, or two swings: out and back again? We breathe in and breathe out in a continuous breath. The outbreath turns into its opposite and back again. In one breath each outbreath, by its very action, makes way for the inbreath, and the inbreath is but a preparation for, or prologue to, the outbreath. All is one and each has its place; a turning wheel of birth and death, or birth/death. Sometimes the alternation is checked or delayed in a leap to growth and evolution, or in a drop to destruction and revolution. Sometimes it is held up and there is war, a dance of death to a symphony of terror. Sometimes alternation is not possible; but how can the universe stop dead in its course?

The turning wheel, the rippling wave; the immovable gives way to the irresistible, which in its turn again becomes the immovable. The one returns to the two, the two to the manifold, the manifold to the One. The whole universe is an unobstructed universe. Why then are there walls and barriers? Why this turning and returning?

Out of the turning wheel arises the center,[6] the point without dimension or location. The center is our point of departure, and our point of arrival. Without the center we have no point in life and become disappointed. Is this a play of words? "What is the point?" we ask. "What is the meaning?" Meaning and the point here are synonymous.

Ambiguity is two extremes in the embrace of Oneness, an embrace that can be the embrace of death through the struggle of eat or be eaten. The embrace then becomes an engulfment of me-as-*center* by me-as-*periphery* and vice versa. Ambiguity then becomes opposition and conflict. The center brings peace; it brings a point around which the two can revolve, a wheel of birth and death. The center is the meaning shared by two extremes. It is Oneness underlying twoness. The center or point is position without content. Meaning is two-becoming-one, a unique center of gravity around which ambiguity swirls, and the embrace of death becomes the dance of life around a still point.

> At the still point of the turning world,
> Neither flesh nor fleshless;
> Neither from nor towards; at the still point, there the dance is.
> But neither arrest nor movement. And do not call it fixity,

> Where past and future are gathered. Neither move-
> ment from nor towards,
> Neither ascent nor decline. Except for the point, the
> still point,
> There would be no dance, and there is only the
> dance.[7]

> —T.S. Eliot

Mumon asked, "If you removed the wheels and took away the axle, then what would it be?" If you took away the still point of the turning world, then what? This magnetic center is all.

> Center, how you draw to yourself out of all things, re-
> gaining yourself even from things in flight: Center
> strongest of all! [8]

> —Rilke

> Self-knowledge reveals the fact that the soul's natural
> movement is not in a straight line. On the contrary, it
> circles around a center.[9]

> —Plotinus

Disappointment is the beginning of practice. When the point of life has been lost, then we can walk into that dark valley of death, of confusion, which is the outcome of an ambiguity so basic that it can no longer be identified as ambiguity. It is only when the axle has been removed that the swinging clash of opposites is no longer held at bay and we have the opportunity to break out of the prison of life, logic, and experience. But to live a life without meaning, to have a wheel without a hub, is this not madness?[10]

The unique center is both what I am *and* that to which I belong: it is the same center, now called "I," now "it." An American and an Eskimo were out during a snowstorm which obliterated all landmarks and so made it difficult to return home. After some time the American said, "We are lost." The Eskimo said, "We are not lost, igloo lost." The center is not subjective, although it is always *my* center; it is not objective, although others may (or rather, *must*) acknowledge it. Although unique, it is jealous, and if not acknowledged, fear and disorientation will occur. In the universe of dynamic interacting and clashing forces of tension *there can be but one center,* there can be no other.

A Raja Yoga teacher said, "Between the eyebrows is a garden in the shape of a cross. At the center of this cross grows a flower. In the center of the flower is a seed, and at the center of the seed, a point. At the center of the point is that which I am."[11] What is that?

Time and again the point, the center recur in human experience. A modern Sufi writer, for example, says, "Whenever I speak of the Point I mean the essence which is named *Oneness of Perception.*"[12] Carl Jung quotes a number of writers who wrote or spoke about the point. One, for example, wrote that one must "above all consider the point in nature and you need nothing else." Jung quotes Monoimos as saying that the point (or as he called it, the jot or tittle) "is the emblem of the complete man. This one tittle is the uncompounded, simple monad, having its composition from nothing whatever, yet composed of many forms, many parts. That simple indivisible joy is the many faced, thousand eyed and thousand armed."[13]

The author Simone Weil wrote in one of her notebooks, "Something infinitely small operates in a decisive manner. There is no mass so heavy but that a given point is equal to it. For a mass will not fall if a single point is upheld, provided that this point is the *center of gravity*" (emphasis added).[14]

A modern writer, George Leonard, says, "In an

expanding universe our own galaxy seems exactly at the center—*and so does every other galaxy.* Every point in this expanding universe acts as if it were at the very center of the universe. This might sound impossible, but the mathematics on the subject is quite clear."[15]

> Though the soul sink all in the oneness of divinity, she never touches bottom. God has left her one little point to get back to herself and know herself as creature.[16]

This point is pure magic. It is the center of all. With it we give life to all and free ourselves from doubt and fear, vanguards of the primal terror coming from the fundamental split of viewpoint which can only be single. This point, this unique center, is what is most dear to me, yet it is only in bestowing it that I come to be. This point is the central value from which all subsequent values are derived. It has been an obsession of mankind and from the most ancient times its symbol has been ☉, the symbol of the sun and of gold. The transmutation of lead into gold was nothing other than the purification of the center, transmuting *I* am into I am. "I am" is our birthright; *"I* am" is our liberator, but it is also our prison.

The center is vital not only to human beings, but to animals, birds, and fish as well.[17] An animal's territory has both boundary (periphery) and center. As an animal retreats toward the center, it gains in psychological strength, and on the other hand loses this strength as it moves away from the center. This is why the neighbor's dog will run after you only for a certain distance.

The question of why animals establish territory is still debated among ethologists. It is obviously not to ensure adequate food supply because some animals leave their territory to find food. It is not to ensure adequate dispersal of the species because establishing territory may create overcrowding. So why is it that a bird, for example, which all winter was content to be an anonymous member of a flock, suddenly leaves its companions and isolates itself to set up territory? Why does this bird, content to live peacefully with others till now, suddenly turn into a martinet, attacking any other of its species daring to trespass upon its territory? It is true that nesting and mating are essential for the continuation of the species, but that may not be all that is involved. If sexuality is the release into Oneness for human beings, is it not also possible that it is so for animals? Territory may not only be that by which the species survives, but also that by which it expresses uniqueness through each individual bird's being the center, and one wonders whether ego is therefore introjected territory.

Birdsong is a means of warning would-be intruders that territory has been taken, just as the dog's bark warns strangers to beware. But is that all? Anyone who is sensitive to a dog will confirm that there is a whole range of communication possible for a dog: anger, supplication, excitement, fear, joy, sorrow. Therefore, while it is difficult to challenge the view that some birdsong may be the means to proclaim territory, nevertheless the questions nags: why has mankind responded so positively to birdsong? Could it be that the Darwinian theory of the struggle for survival is only half the story and that *survival* (or preservation) of *uniqueness* has a twin in *the expression of uniqueness?* If so, would not the center of territory be the first fundamental expression of this uniqueness and that by which the power of Oneness, mana, is earthed? Center, sexuality, song, and ego: all manifestations of One at play.

Primitive villages were often constructed with a center and boundary. At the center there was a plaza, an area for festive and public life, a sacred area that included the burial ground. In other villages the men's house was at the center and this house in turn had a center such as a chimney or a sacred tree.

The sacred tree as the cosmic center, world center, or world navel is universal, and it later developed into the totem pole of the Indians and the church spire of the Christians. The Christmas tree is a degenerate cosmic center, the angel at the top being an echo of the soul or god that was thought to inhabit the tree. The candles and tinsel were once the numinous aura that surrounded the tree and the gifts evidence of the tree's bounty. The cosmic tree was considered to be the center of the three worlds and one gained access to these worlds via this center. Some trees had seven branches by which a shaman ascended to heaven.

Sometimes the symbolism of the chimney and the tree are combined during festivities, the tree now standing at the center of the men's house and protruding through the chimney. The legend of Santa Claus gaining access to a house via the chimney possibly owes its origins to this or similar beliefs. In some myths there is a serpent at the root of the tree and an eagle at its summit, engaged in perpetual war with each other. This emphasizes the role of the tree as a center reconciling antagonistic viewpoints.

Buddhism too has its sacred trees. Buddha was born under a tree, he came to awakening under a tree, and he died under a tree. In Nepal two trees, the pipal tree and the banyan tree, are planted together. As they grow, their trunks join into a single tree, the join becoming indistinguishable even to an experienced forester, while the branches remain distinctive to the respective species. They are between them a "sacred" tree and a special platform is built around the tree so that weary travellers can find rest in its shade. Tradition has it that Buddha sat under the pipal tree when he came to awakening, and then sat under the banyan tree, the symbol of worldly knowledge.

Some writers have seen an analogy between the cosmic tree and the Christian cross of crucifixion.

> The Buddha beneath the tree of awakening (the Bo
> tree) and Christ on the Holy Rood (tree of redemp-
> tion) are analogous figures, incorporating an arche-
> typal world saviour, world tree motif, which is of
> immemorial antiquity. . . . The immovability of Bud-
> dha and the uniqueness of the world center symbol-
> ized by the tree coincide.[18]

Not only are trees considered to be the center of the world, but mountains also share in this position of honor—Mount Meru, Mount Olympus, Golgotha, Mount Tabor in Palestine, Mount Fuji, and so on. Furthermore, "north" means center for all the tribes in Asia with the North Pole being the center of the sky. Indeed, ultimately, as Mircea Eliade points out, every human habitation is projected to the center of the world.[19] "The hearth in the home, the altar in the temple, is the hub of the wheel of the earth, the womb of the universal mother whose fire is the fire of life. And the opening at the top of the lodge (men's house) or the crown pinnacle or the lantern of the dome is the hub or midpoint of the sky."[20]

If it is true that each "habitation is projected to the center of the world," why are there so many myths and rituals concerned with the difficulties, and overcoming the difficulties, of reaching the center? For example, Mecca is the holy city of Islam. As most people know, the faithful prostrate themselves periodically during the day, while facing toward Mecca. At these times Mecca is at the center of millions of Moslems, all facing inward toward the holy center. Mecca is also the center to which the faithful periodically travel on pilgrimage, and at these times hundreds of thousands of people of all ages stream from all directions. Many of the pilgrims walk to Mecca and some impose additional hardships upon themselves, perhaps crawling for hundreds of miles, or carrying heavy loads. Why do they do this if their own home is the center?

Jerusalem was "the holy city not simply as the place made forever illustrious by the Advent, Passion, and Ascension of Christ, but also as the navel of the world, the land fruitful above all others, like another paradise of delights, the city placed in the center of the world."[21]

Possibly one of the most celebrated of modern Buddhist pilgrims was Hsu-yun, who went on a pilgrimage to a holy mountain, traveling the entire distance of more than a thousand miles walking three steps, then making a full prostration.

But the question remains: why the pilgrimage to the center? Each of us is the center, the center which is a viewpoint. This viewpoint is the entry of Oneness in communion with itself, and as such it is the most mysterious and miraculous, while being the most obvious and commonplace, event. Whenever we wonder, whenever we crave magic, the numinous, the transcendent, it is the evocation of this first mystery that we seek.

However, at the same time, the viewpoint is of something. What this *something* is makes no difference, but now *it*, this something, is the center. This something could simply be a thought, even the thought of a thought, but it is the One incarnate, with all the strength and power of the One.

When that something is another viewpoint, this strength and power become both a threat and a promise. Oneness is therefore evoked once again, this time as a reconciler, a center of a dynamic field, a world center.[22]

This world center has to be established with great care, reverence, labor, and pain: the pain of sacrifice and the labor of work. This is the pain and labor of religion. But in that this center is unique, in that people make it "my center," then it becomes a cause for dissension. Such a claim is necessary and inevitable, just as the pain and the labor to reach and establish the center is necessary and inevitable.

There is an ancient story that Joseph Campbell tells in his book *The Hero with a Thousand Faces*. He introduces the story with the following:

> The world navel is ubiquitous. Ugliness and beauty, sin and virtue, pleasure and pain are equally its production. However, the figures worshipped in the temples of the world are not always good and likewise mythology does not have as its greatest hero the merely virtuous man.

He goes on: A tribe in east Africa has a trickster divinity named Edshu. One day Edshu was walking along a path between two fields in each of which a farmer was at work. Edshu decided to play a trick on these farmers and put on a hat that was red on one side, white on the other, green in front, and black behind. These colors, symbolic of the four directions, indicate that Edshu was at the center, the *axis mundi* or world navel.

When the two farmers returned home, one said to the other, "Did you see that fellow in the white hat go by?" His companion said, "But it was not white, it was red." The first retorted, "No, you are wrong, it was white." "Impossible," said the other, "it was red—I saw it with my own eyes." "You've got to be blind," said the first. "And you must be drunk," said the other. The argument developed until the two came to blows. When they drew knives, the neighbors decided to step in, and they brought the antagonists before the head man for judgment. "Edshu was among the crowd at the trial, and when the head man sat at a loss to know where justice lay, the old trickster revealed himself, made known his prank, and showed the hat. 'The two could not help but quarrel,' he said, 'I wanted it that way. Spreading strife is my greatest joy.'"[23]

We should not wonder at the farmers fighting: is the hat of the trickster figure, the ubiquitous center, red or white? Suppose he carried a flag: was it the red, white, and blue of the British, or the white and blue of the Argentines? Does he speak Russian or English? Did he vote conservative or liberal? Does the center unite or divide? Bring peace or a sword?

Is this talk of centers confusing? First we talked of a center which I am: the original viewpoint. Simultaneously another center, that which I am peripheral to, sprang into being. Now we have a third center which is unique, but which is everywhere, which unites, but divides; which is sacred, but without conscience. Is there one center, two centers, or three centers? Is it all a figment of the imagination? Does it matter? These are important questions. To help answer them, let us consider the story of Renée.

Renée was a young French girl who at an early age became schizophrenic. She was subsequently cured of her schizophrenia and wrote her autobiography, a short but moving account of what it feels like to be schizophrenic.[24]

Schizophrenia means "split" mind or personality. A well-known writer on this and other subjects says that a schizophrenic becomes such through living in an environment in which a conflict is generated that has to be resolved but cannot be resolved. The situation, it is felt, is created by someone giving conflicting commands, accompanied by a threat of punishment if both are not complied with.[25] Does this not sound like the center/periphery dilemma that was outlined earlier? I am the center, but because of that I am not the center, yet because I am an individual I have to be either one or the other, but also because I am an individual and whole, I cannot be one or the other as these are only "halves" and therefore I have to be both.

The solution to this human double bind is arrived at through the magic or sacred center. This is unique as it is "my" center, or equally well it could be said to be my center because it is unique. It is objective because others can attest to its uniqueness; it is central because ultimately everything stands in relation to it and thus it is the point at which all conflict is reconciled. Sometimes it is called "I," sometimes "it." Because it reconciles conflict it relieves us of our human burden of pain; it is a vehicle for our precious uniqueness and the way out of our intolerable ambiguity.

But what if for one reason or another this magic center loses its magical energy of Oneness; what if the mana is not there? If the center is lost amid millions of centers, engulfed in the universe like a needle lost in a haystack, where one thing is as good as another, where would be the uniqueness? Where would be the center? This was the case with Renée. A frequent and recurring dream that she had was of just this terror. She dreamed of a barn

> . . . brilliantly illuminated by electricity. The walls
> painted white, smooth and shining. In the immensity,
> a needle—fine, pointed, hard, glittering in the light.
> The needle in the emptiness filled me with excruciat-
> ing terror. Then a haystack fills up the emptiness and
> engulfs the needle. The haystack, small at first, swells
> and swells and in the center the needle, endowed
> with tremendous electrical force, communicates its
> charge to the hay. The blinding light, the electrical cur-

rent, the invasion by the hay combine to augment the
fear to a paroxysm of terror and I wake up screaming,
"the needle, the needle."[26]

The needle is the center, the electrical current is
mana, the energy of oneness-which-is-two. The hay is
swamping the needle. Renée's dream is of the loss of the
magic center and *this loss exposes her to the
irreconcilable opposition of being both at the center
and the periphery,* with all the terror and horror of the
self devouring the self. The bright light we are also
familiar with, although when encountered through love
it has as its accompaniment beatitude and bliss.

Renée's struggle was to establish and maintain a
center. The psychoanalyst perceived the nature of this
struggle and offered herself as center, as *mama.* "Little
Renée need not be afraid when there's Mama. She is
stronger than anything else. . ."

Renée reports, "What did me the most amazing
amount of good was her use of the third person in
speaking of herself: Mama and Renée, not I and you."[27]
"I," as we said, is the name of the magic center. "I" and
"you" set up an opposition, and it was precisely this
intolerable opposition that Renée could not stand.
"Mama" and "Renée" were "out there," objective,
united, central. "Mama I recognized less and less; in her
place I recognized the Queen, the Goddess, source
of life and joy."[28]

When Mama was not there to be the center, "for the
greater part of the day I sat in a chair gazing fixedly
before me or plunged in the absorbed contemplation of
a tiny spot: a spot which, no bigger than a grain of
pepper, could hold me for an hour without any urge to
shift my eyes from this absorption in the microscopic
world."[29]

The inability to establish a center had, of course, a

corresponding inability to establish "I," and the cure of Renée was associated with relearning the word "I." "I permitted myself to say 'my body, I am washing it, I am pretty.'"[30]

The inability to establish "I" led to other problems. For example: "Sometimes I did not know clearly whether it was she or I who needed something. For instance, if I asked for another cup of tea and Mama asked teasingly, 'But why do you want more tea; don't you see I have just finished my cup and so you don't need any?' Then I replied, 'Yes, that's true. I don't need any more,' confusing herself with me. But at bottom I did desire a second cup of tea and suddenly in a flash I realized that Mama's satiety did not make me satisfied too."[31]

Does it not become more clear why it is that the magic center called ego is so important, and why, for example, the German people during the chaotic times of the Weimar Republic found Hitler the unique center of the universe?

As stress increases there is an increase in anxiety and this may lead to fear and eventually to panic. People lost in a forest in which one tree looks like all other trees and so none is unique and therefore the center, have been known to break down in panic. Consider an army facing battle. Pain, mutilation, death threaten. From all sides noise, confusion, and chaos flood in. What could there be to hold men together, to give them strength and unity? On the one hand, there is the Oneness of discipline, the ritual of marching in step, exercising together, dressing uniformly; on the other hand, there is the flag.

The flag is a magic center, its magic bestowed by the leader who, when the flag is brought into his or her presence, bestows mana. Each year in Britain there is a ceremony in which the flags of the British regiments are brought within the presence of the monarch. The ceremony is called "Trooping the Color." A similar ceremony was held in Nazi Germany at Nuremburg when Hitler would "consecrate" new party colors. He would touch them with one hand while his other hand clutched the cloth of the bullet-riddled "Blutfahne" (the "blood banner" allegedly drenched in the gore of Nazi martyrs killed in the abortive putsch of November 1923).

A flag is found prominently displayed on the parade ground of a barracks or on the quarterdeck of a ship. Various ceremonies are conducted for the raising and lowering of the flag morning and evening, with special music, some of it very haunting, and special drills and salutes. The flag is treated with the utmost respect, and punishment for desecrating a flag was once severe. The flag is carried at the head of any parade and is always displayed prominently. At one time it was enough for an army to capture the standard for the enemy to be routed. The standard bearer was chosen from amongst the bravest. As long as the flag was flying, a stable center existed, but as soon as it was gone the opposites were no longer held at bay and panic and terror resulted.

The flag is not only a center for an army, but for whole nations as well. During the Falklands crisis the then President of Argentina was interviewed on television and presumably watching was Margaret Thatcher, the British Prime Minister. A writer commenting on the interview said, "Two words that Margaret Thatcher heard on the TV filled her with cold fury and determination to win." What were these two words? Galtieri seemed ready to accommodate in the cause of a peaceful solution. He even conceded that sovereignty, which up till then had been *the* issue, would no longer be a precondition for cease-fire and peace talks. Then he was asked if he would agree that the flag of Argentina should, at least temporarily, be lowered on the Falkland Islands? "There was a pause, the benign look abruptly vanished. The presidential lips hardened to a thin line and spat out the words, 'No, señor!'"[32]

Transference of mana or the power of the center is also made possible through sacred relics. Bones, parts of the cross, and other relics of Christ or martyred saints, of Buddha and patriarchs are made into relics and housed in churches and temples. The Buddhist stupa in which sacred relics are enshrined is an elaborate sacred tree or world center.[33]

This transference of the unique center is not paradoxical because uniqueness is bestowed and not found. If a tree is sacred it is so because uniqueness has been bestowed upon it. The tree is unique because of uniqueness, not because of being a tree. However, the identification of the tree with uniqueness is a fundamental illusion. The magic center has to be fixed and immutable; otherwise it is not the center, but when it is fixed in any kind of form it becomes a stake to which we are tied.

> One day when Ma-tsu, a great Zen master, was walking with Po-chang, his disciple, a flock of wild geese flew overhead.
> Ma-tsu asked Po-chang, "What is there?"
> Po-chang replied, "Wild geese."
> Ma-tsu asked, "Where are they now?"
> Po-chang replied, "They have flown away."
> Ma-tsu seized Po-chang's nose and gave it a violent twist so that Po-chang cried out in pain.[34]

Why does Ma-tsu go on like this? Don't these geese come and go?

> When Tung-shan came to Yun-men the master asked him, "Where are you from?"

"From Ch'a tsu, sir!"

"Where were you during the summer?"

"Pao-tsu monastery in Hunan."

"When did you leave there?"

"The eighth of August."

"I absolve you from thirty blows!"[33]

But why the absolution? What is wrong?

In a Buddhist temple or *zendo* (meditation hall) there is always an altar with a figure, usually Buddha, prominently displayed. The altar is the visual and dynamic center of the room and usually the first thing seen on entering. It is frequently lit more brightly than other parts of the room; it is aesthetically pleasing and as the dynamic center all activities are made with reference to it. One bows to the altar on entering the zendo and during the various rituals.

Being at the center and being the highest are seen to be the same; therefore bowing is a way of yielding the center to that to which the bow is directed. A full prostration, or lying full-length facedown before the altar, as is done for example by monks before a Christian altar, raises the altar to its highest and therefore makes it absolute as a center.

In a zendo the teacher, before giving a *teisho* will prostrate a number of times before the Buddha, and make offerings of incense. He does not face the students when giving the teisho but instead faces Buddha. This, and the bows, ensure that the Buddha, rather than the teacher, is the center. In turn this helps clean the teacher of his own feelings of uniqueness, and helps clean the students of their tendency—indeed, in some it is more an ardent desire—to see the teacher as center.

The Buddha figure is a religious figure and strictly speaking it is Buddha. This is constantly emphasized by Kapleau-roshi whenever he makes reference to the

Buddha on the altar. It is not an ornament, nor a work of art, but an "object" of religion. It therefore has the same status as a sacred tree or sacred mountain in that it is the center of the universe, the cosmic center. The Buddha now becomes the unique center and so one is freed of the burden of the search for it. While paying obeisance to the Buddha there is a release from the suffering caused by a center which is forever transient and elsewhere, and the wandering of the center is laid to rest.

What is the difference between the flag and a Buddha or a crucifix? That the flag is a sacred object for many is without doubt.

> With an impulsive gesture he reached out and, catching hold of the flag in his hand, kissed it. For the moment the faithful were stunned, at the spontaneity, the beauty and love, the unexpectedness of the gesture. Then there burst forth, as from all persons become One, a mighty shout of reverent delight, which echoed and re-echoed around the lofty vaulting of the Basilica. One felt the presence of a gigantic superhuman power, as wave after wave of passionate emotions swept the multitude.[36]

This time "he" was the Pope, the flag he touched was the French flag.

The reverence toward the flag and an altar is the same and it is different. It is the "difference" of course that makes the difference, *but when this difference is not there, then the reverence toward the flag and altar is the same, no matter whether that altar is in a church or temple, Christian or Buddhist.* What is this difference?

Buddha means *awakened,* awakened from the dream of a unique center. *In awakening, samadhi, or enlightenment, there is no unique center.* This gives the impression, for example, that the universe is unobstructed. There are countless koans that attest to the centerlessness of samadhi. For example:

> During a snowfall Layman P'ang was walking to the gates of a temple accompanied by some monks "Beautiful snowflakes falling nowhere," he said.[37]

> "What is the most holy truth?" asked Emperor Wu of Bodhidharma. "Vast emptiness, no holiness."[38]

Furthermore the Zen masters are merciless toward all Buddhist iconography. There is the famous story of the Zen master who, on a cold night, visited a temple in which the priest was obviously attached to his Buddha figures. When the priest left the room for a moment the Zen master grabbed one of the figures and threw it on the fire. When the priest came back he found to his horror the Zen master warming his hands by a burning Buddha. "What are you doing?" the priest shouted. "I'm looking for the sarira,"* replied the master. Rinzai exclaimed, "If you meet the Buddha, kill him!"

Mumon, in his comments on the koans, uses irony to dethrone not only Shakyamuni Buddha and Maitreya, but all the Zen masters as well.

Why this onslaught? Furthermore, why did Gutei cut off the boy's finger? Why does Zen master Baso first say, "Mind is Buddha" and then "No Mind, no Buddha"? Another master said, "Progress made by concentration is still a delusion. Because the mind is bound by concentration, concentration itself becomes a hindrance of good karma. If there is even a tiny spot of impurity in the mind, this imperfection is conceived of as ignorance."[39] Why is this?

---

* Sarira are small hard deposits that remain from the ashes of a wise man and are evidence of his holiness. They appear around the neck and are called Buddha's necklace. They are highly prized relics. The master was asking, "How can this piece of wood be a sacred center?"

The flag is the center, but the center is not the flag. Buddha is the center, but the center is not Buddha. When one makes obeisance to the Buddha, this acknowledges Buddha as the unique center. When Mumon uses irony to dethrone the Buddha, he says that the center is not Buddha.

Hubert Benoit, in his book *The Supreme Doctrine,* gives a parable of a fox who, to divest itself of fleas, enters a stream tail first. The fleas all hop forward until the fox is immersed, all but the nose. Then it dips its nose into the water. During a teisho a teacher will say in all kinds of ways that there is no unique center, or, which is the same thing, everything is a unique center, even dung—*all the while facing the unique center.*

> A monk asked, "Among the manifold forms of appearance, what is the pure essence of things?"
> "All are," said the master.[40]

The same master, Wen-i, said, "Among all manifestations the Solitary One is revealed. Why should you speak of disregarding them or not?"[41]

Time and again Zen masters warn against just sitting and sinking into a void. They call this the cave of demons and the deep pit of pseudo-emancipation. Zen is not simply a question of letting go of the magic center. Nor is it a question of concentration, of simply bringing the mind to one-pointedness.

In the Surangama Sutra, Buddha warns his disciples of confusing the moon with the finger that points to the moon; or of confusing Buddha with the Buddha figure, or Oneness with Oneness incarnate as the unique center. But can we do without the finger, the Buddha figure on the altar, the unique center?

> A monk said, "As for the finger, I will not ask you

about it. But what is the moon?" The master asked, "Where is the finger that you do not ask about?" So the monk asked, "As for the moon, I will not ask about it. But what is the finger?" The master said, "The moon." The monk challenged him and said, "I asked about the finger, why do you answer me the moon?" "Because you asked me about the finger."[42]

It could be said that there are two kinds of religion: one that gives a center, another that takes it away. The first is a religion that gives meaning, a direction to life, a purpose for living. Someone said, "We all need something to believe in." Another said, "If God did not exist, we would have to invent him."

And the second kind of religion—

Gettan said to a monk, "Keichu made a hundred carts. If you took off the wheels and removed the axle, then what would it be?"

7

The Center: Friend or Foe?

Goso said, "To give an example, it is like a cow going through a window: its head, horns, and four legs all pass through—why doesn't its tail, too?"[1]

What is stopping the cow's tail from going through the window? A Zen master said, "The absolute moment of waving a finger (or tail) does what all the disciplines of the world can do." Some people misconstrue this and say that therefore it is really quite easy. But this same teacher said in the next breath, "If one would follow this way, how much effort one must put into it!"

Why will the tail not pass through? What is stopping it? It is, after all, not much—just a tiny tip.

It is like trying to find a picnic spot. This place would be fine, but there are some ants; what a shame it is that that spot is so much in the sun; we could stop here, but then we'd be so close to that noisy group; now we have lost the view—that's bad luck because this spot is just perfect otherwise.

The word *duhkha* is often translated as suffering, and the first noble truth of Buddhism, its basic axiom, is that suffering is universal. But it is not always suffering as such, but rather a deep uneasiness, a kind of spiritual discomfort. The opposite of duhkha is *sukha*—happiness. Sukha meant originally a well-centered hub, and duhkha would then mean a wheel that was slightly off center, a constant bumping and grating: the job is fine, but my boss, well, he's a bit difficult; the house is just right, but there's a bus stop just outside the door; my marriage is really great, but, . . . the holiday is fine, except. . . .

Mumon's verse to this koan reads:

> If it passes through, it falls into a ditch.
> If it turns back, it is destroyed.
> This tiny tail, how marvelous.[2]

Duhkha also means twoness: *duh* "two," *kha* "ness." There is that uneasy feeling of having to do something but not wanting to do it; of wanting to do something, but being unable to—the nagging feeling of being damned if one does and damned if one doesn't—the muffled feeling that one ought to speak up, but not wanting to be "pushy"; of wanting to leave, but not wanting to be thought a coward. And so one stays in a job, knowing one should leave, and then leaves it while feeling it would have been better to stay. Change is fearful, but what is, is no good. Caught on the horns of boredom and insecurity, bondage and uncertainty, one goes around and around, but off center, pulling and pushing—while the tail remains stuck. Even our best moments, caught as they are in the sparkle of sunlight and laughter, giving peace and rest at last, are moments in time leading to sunset, when the wind springs up and the others leave and go home, and peace and rest go with them.

What must we do? Look on the bright side? Grin and bear it, count our blessings? But if we do, we must turn our back upon that elusive dream of hope. Or is it some nostalgic ghost that beckons from the shadows of our mind, inviting us to a fuller life, without compromise—to a life even beyond light and space and laughter.

So we attack, take up arms against a sea of troubles, thrash at the cobwebs of inertia, make resolutions, intentions, efforts toward a new life, reborn and resurrected. The laughter gets louder, and feet run away down the corridors of our mind; we're left with a vague feeling of having failed, of having betrayed something or someone—ourself, perhaps, or the light and space and laughter. We try to fall in love, try to improve ourselves, to do some good, but it is all such an effort. Pull, push, strain, stretch—the tail stays stuck.

Even when we have achieved success, respectability, and status; have gained knowledge, proven by degrees; have traveled, gained experience, helped people; have got the head, body, and four legs through—yet there is the tail, the tip of the tail! But, as Mumon says, "How marvelous!"

Krishnamurti, a well-known contemporary teacher, asks in one of his many books, "Can the center be still, or can the center fade away? Can the center be completely absorbed, dissolved, or lie as a fragment in the distance? If there is no possibility of that, then I must accept prison."[3] Is this what is required? Must the tail fade away, be completely absorbed, or even be forever still? The tail brushes away the flies. What good would a tail that couldn't move be to a cow? Can we live without a center? If human beings have worked so hard to establish a center, have gone on myriads of pilgrimages to find the center, have fought so desperately to defend the center, are we now to just let it fade away, be absorbed, or lie as a fragment?

Dogen said that working on onself takes sweat, tears, and sometimes blood. Almost all authentic religions have had the notion of death and rebirth, the death of the old man and the birth of the new: death and resurrection. What is this death? Why is it so painful and why does the struggle to come to awakening require that we pass through the dark night of the soul, through the valley of the shadow of death?

> A special transmission outside the scriptures, not founded upon words and letters; by pointing directly to man's own mind it lets him see into his own true nature and thus attain Buddhahood.[4]

Got it! Like the flash of a cat whose long wait is rewarded, we flash onto the back of the tired mouse as it skitters across the floor. Words! There's the demon. Words and letters are the enemy. There has to be an enemy, a spiritual virus, something to be purged, cauterized, eliminated, or got rid of, and words are it! We knew it all along; get rid of words and thoughts, and the tail will spring free.

Or will it?

"All words belong to the demons!" said Yang-shan, a monk who had just come to awakening. The master was so delighted by this answer that he said to his disciple, "Hereafter nobody will be able to do anything to you!"

But if words are from the devil, would we not all be better off as deaf-mutes? Let us ask Helen Keller, a deaf-mute, who was blind as well. She wrote:

> Someone was drawing water and my teacher placed my hand under the spout. As the cool stream gushed over my hand she spelled into the other the word

w-a-t-e-r, first slowly, and then rapidly. I stood still, my whole attention fixed upon the motion of her fingers. Suddenly I felt a misty consciousness as of something forgotten, . . . and somehow the mystery of language was revealed to me. I knew then that w-a-t-e-r meant the wonderful cool something that was flowing over my hand. That living word awakened my soul, gave it light, hope, set it free.[5]

One word was all that was necessary and a girl imprisoned in darkness, silence, and loneliness was set free. One word for freedom, but words are from the devil? Is the tail stuck again? Mumon is unequivocal: "When the mouth opens, all are wrong." The evangelist St. John is equally unequivocal: "In the beginning was the Word and the Word was with God and *the Word was God.*"

If the Word was God, how can it belong to the devil? The word is God not only for the Christians, but for the ancient Aryans also. In the Rig Veda the Word as God says:

> Through my power he eats and sees,
> Breathes and hears.
> Who hears me as Vac (the Word)
> Even if they do not know, they dwell in me.
> In truth I speak: hear me, famous men.[6]

Through the power of the word, the world is revealed to us, action becomes possible, even for those not aware of this. The Third Patriarch, on the other hand, says, "Cut off all useless thoughts and words and there's nowhere you cannot go."

Who is right, who is wrong? Did we pounce too hastily on the wee beastie? Is the word Dr. Jekyll or Mr. Hyde?

Oswald Spengler says, "The mere creation of the name *time* was an unparalleled deliverance."[7] This echoes Helen Keller's sentiments somewhat. Language is, some say, the first gift of the gods; others say that it is the greatest of all man's creations, for after all, are not science, philosophy, literature, even religion cradled, nurtured, and supported by language? But a Zen master insists, "Words cannot explain the real nature of the universe. Only common people, fettered with desire, make use of this arbitrary method." Walt Whitman must not have encountered Zen because he said, "All words are spiritual."

A Catholic priest, an exorcist, said, "It was a considerable victory to obtain the devils' names, as they customarily refused to give them unless forced to it by a stronger will or by the invocation of the holy names, whereupon the unhappy victims seemed plunged into the tortures of the damned."[8]

To control the devil you have to name him: this is an old adage of magic. How can words then be from the devil?

How can anything be so blessed and so cursed? It would seem that in words we have come to the ultimate Janus.

A monk asked, "To become one with reality directly, one should speak non-dual words. What are non-dual words?" The master said, "How can you add any more?"

If we are going to speak of Oneness and all words are dual words and Janus-like, how are we to do this? Are all words but metaphors? Does this mean we should take a vow of silence?

A monk asked a master, "Speaking and silence are both half the truth. How can we be free, but without error?" Fuketsu said, "How fondly I remember Konan in March! The partridges are calling and the flowers are fragrant."[9] These were not original words, but a quote from an even earlier poet, and yet they are non-dual words.

Are words the devil?

"Aristotle is dead because he was, more than any other notable writer in the whole history of philosophy, superstitiously devoted to words. Even in his logic he is absolutely dependent on the accident of his mother tongue."[10] Does this give us a clue? Is it only Aristotle who is superstitiously devoted to words?

An Araucanian Indian, asked his name by someone ignorant of his superstition, will answer, "I have none."[11] Who is the superstitious one: the Indian or the one who asks his name?

In the Diamond Sutra it is stated in effect that when the Tathagata uses words, they don't assert any definite or arbitrary idea. He merely uses words as words. How many people can use words as words? But if we do not use words as words, what do we use them as?

"In the beginning was the Word."[12] Long ago some forgotten seer struggled to give expression to the mystery that dumbfounds us all: "How did it all start?" How to account for that first act of creation. And so, it seems, he accounted for it by another creative act, also miraculous, but one repeated each day, the creative act of speech.[13] "In the beginning was the Word." In the beginning, "God said, 'Let there be light.'" Did he say it or sing it? There are some who believe that speech and song were once the same. Did he just sing it, or dance it as well? Recent research seems to show that an intricate, complex but predictable subliminal dance accompanies all that we say and that our listeners dance along with us.[14]

If we try to peer back into the shadows to a time when the first words were said, sung, or danced, we can perhaps faintly sense that awe and wonder of the tribe gathered around the shaman, the living center. He was the man of magic, religion, art, and science, who conveyed to the tribe the mysteries of the cycle of time. It was he who revealed origins and destinies, meanings, wresting from the shadowy demons their power by the light of the word. He named the gods and brought them under control. We can feel the amazement of comprehension as one after the other tribal member grasped the truth, the truth not of some proposition or formula, but the truth of w-a-t-e-r, the truth of the living word that awakens the soul, giving it light and hope and setting it free.

Words and magic have always been associated. The "abracadabra" of the stage conjurer is but the husk of the potency of the seed syllables or mantric words of old. Even today there are many who believe that words have creative value and are "a compelling magic tool for calling up immediate reality."[15] It is this same magic that reveals new relations between ideas or things brought out in a new theory. The word is evocative and calls the world into existence, and so for that brief moment frees us from existence. The poet, the storyteller, and bard, have always had a special place in the hearts of people because the magic of words is not a solitary thing but something that must be shared. It is through words we encounter the Other, not simply the other as trees, flowers, earth, and water, although these too are revealed, but the other as a shared and sharing Other.

Heidegger says, "We are a conversation, conversation supports our existence."[16] "It is precisely in the naming of the gods and in the transmutation of the world into word that the real conversation, which we ourselves are, consists."[17] What can this mean, "We are a conversation"?

There was an elderly woman visiting a museum containing the relics and remains of old ships that once sailed and steamed along and across the rivers and lakes

of Canada. She was in deep conversation with someone
of whom she was obviously fond. She would talk, laugh,
turn away coyly, and come back engaging and intimate.
Familiar, gentle, and loving toward the other person and
talking all the time, she walked around the museum,
alone. We invited her for a cup of tea in the museum's
restaurant and she told us of her young days, when she
was a girl; how she used to steam down the river, with
all the gleaming brass and polished woodwork around,
sometimes taking the wheel. And she told how her
father, the ship's captain, would explain to her all sorts
of things, bringing the world into being, calling up trees,
birds, fish with names, and with names opening up a
future and fashioning a past. But was that all she saw? Or
did she also see, revealed and revealing, the Other,
which in her love was simply her own face—her father as
the Other, her father as herself, herself as center, herself
as periphery. As we talked to her, we knew that the
conversation with her father must go on. If he were to
die, the light would go from the world, the Other would
leave, and she too would leave through the doors of
madness or of death.

In twoness we find ourselves as one. "The oneness of
conversation," says Heidegger, "consists of the fact that
in the essential word there is always that one and same
thing on which we agree, and on the basis of which we
are united and are essentially ourselves."[18]

> Ejaku, a celebrated Zen master, asked Enen, "What is
> your name?" Enen, another Zen master, said, "Ejaku."
> Ejaku said, "Ejaku is my name." Enen said, "My name
> is Enen." Ejaku roared with laughter.[19]

I am a conversation, it is through the Other that I have
my being, and it is through words, sung or spoken,
danced or mimed, that I come to others. As center there

is me, as periphery there is you; as center there is you, as periphery there is me. Giving and taking, we are two but one; talking and listening, I am one but two. Our whole world comes out of the word that was in the beginning, a word that was both "I" and "Thou."[20]

But then I claim to be the center and as such to express the One Mind as the unique one. Conversation becomes opposing monologues, held together by the need to dominate in argument, and I deceive others and am deceived by them. It is only when *I* cease to be that I and Thou can dance our dance of Oneness again.

> After extinction I came out, and I
> Eternal now am though not as *I*
> Yet who am *I*, Oh I, but *I?*[21]
>
> I am the silence that is incomprehensible.
> I am the utterance of my name.[22]

The silence and the utterance: in the beginning was the Word. A monk asked Hogen, "My name is Echo. I ask you, what is Buddha?" Hogen said, "You are Echo."[23] A word, a name—"water," "time," "tail," "ox," "God," "Devil," "Echo,"—brings the whole world into being. The word is God because God is the silence that is incomprehensible and the utterance of his name. Consciousness and name, says the Buddhist sage, are the cause of each other, each brings the other into being; the silence as utterance, the utterance as silence. Form as emptiness, emptiness as form.

The fabric of consciousness, then, is woven from words. The whole tapestry of our existence is made of words, of which the center is the weaver. The center does not "exist"; it is the attempt to evoke the center that calls existence into being. It is like a ball rolling around a plate that is being tilted this way and that. The ball is seeking the center, which always remains constant as the center. The ball and the plate change their relation, like dancers on a stage, choreographed around a stable center. But the ball is always overshooting the mark, its very momentum works against it. Always it is forced to retrace its roll, but it can never do so exactly because the plate has already tilted to a new plane. Only accidentally does it cross the center in a brief moment of revelation and for that brief moment it becomes the center. Thus it might be said of experience and existence: the one moving in relation to the other, seeking the center. The moments of revelation bring new words into being, words which are the concentration of Oneness into a single point at the center of gravity of all.

The association of the point and language is brought out vividly in the mystical teachings of the Hebrews and Sufis: "The light burst forth from the mystery of emptiness. The hidden point was manifest: that is the letter Yod."[24] In Hebrew the letter Yod is written as a point and it is from the point that all other letters of Hebrew are formed. Just as the silence is the utterance, so the ink is the point, and the point is the word.

A Sufi poet says, "If you grasp the truth you will see only the ink itself, which is what is meant by the point."[25] "Letters," says another Sufi poet, "are signs of the ink. The color of the letters is an illusion because the color comes from the ink."[26] Words have meaning and power because they point to the center, and it is from the center that meaning and power come. And the center has its power from Oneness reconciling the irreconcilable viewpoint from which arises the basic ambiguity. Words are not the center, because the center cannot exist as words can be said to exist, nor is the center the words. "I am the utterance of my name," because I and the name are different. Form is emptiness because form is form.

From the point come the letters and the names. It is by the name that Oneness is transmuted into uniqueness. In the Lord's Prayer we say, "Hallow'd be thy name." To take the name in vain is to mix it with other names, to make it common by bringing it down to earth. This is blasphemy.

To a townsman all oxen look alike, but to the cowherd each has a name. Everything in our world has a name. As God created, so Adam named. Everything then, through its name, is unique, and when its name is called comes to the center of the stage, a star for a moment. But each of us calls our own name constantly, each claiming to be the superstar in a world where there can be but One.

In Egypt the question arose as to how the first God, the creator Khepera, had come into existence. The answer was given that in the beginning Khepera created himself by calling his own name.[27] Each of us is Khepera, calling ourselves into being with the word "I." I is not the first word in time that we use, but it is the first in importance. "I" which is my name frees me from the bondage of nature. "I" is my first conquest and I become absolute, distinct, separate, and liberated. "My goodness, I am me!"

"I am, none else beside me."[28] "I" is the central word. All values owe allegiance to the center, they point to it and sustain it. All that is good, right, beautiful, and just supports the center; all that is bad, wrong, ugly would destroy it, erode it, or create another in its stead. The center is jealous and can bear no other. "I" usurps that value of the center and the world is named and subordinated by the word and transmuted from the dross of existence into the gold of experience.

But there is an irony in this transmutation: in the very act of naming and subordinating the world by naming, the twin of "I" is born. The world, nature, being can all be reduced to the central word "it."

"Even the same thing seen from two different points of view gives rise to two entirely different descriptions, and descriptions give rise to two entirely different theories, and the theories to two entirely different sets of actions."[29]

We seek a permanent cure for the wound at the heart of our being by trying to get the center into consciousness by words and in so doing create an implacable duality: me and the world, subject and object, self and other, "I" and "it."

And at the same time a third appears. "I" and "it" are separated by an unbridgable gulf, the gulf of "nothing," "not," the ultimate anomaly in a world of Oneness. "The negative," someone said, "is a linguistic marvel."[30] This may be so, but *nothing* is not a mere word, but a byproduct of the "Word."

From "nothing" comes death, seen as extinction or total annihilation, and this death is one of the basic and most painful of all illusions. It is the death that can be died while one is still alive and from which comes the true resurrection.

> If you die before you die
> You do not die when you die.

Once the act of separation has been made, there is no end to it. More and more I am I by not being you or him or her or it. Words have to be defined and redefined to limit their potency so that they are able to better serve in holding the center in place. This creates a new stress. As enemies are created, allies become needed: as "this" is separated from "that," so it becomes necessary to join "this" to "that." We become like cathedrals of tension, with buttresses and arches, columns and supports, thrusts and counterthrusts, in a never-ending juggle designed to restore a lost equilibrium. But like a little child running downhill, the faster he goes, the worse it gets.

Experience is at odds with existence, and we distort the one to match the other; experience hardens and becomes resistant to the frustrations and assaults of existence, while existence is tailored and trimmed to match our conception of how things should be. Our life becomes broken into islands of experience as we act out now the role of father, now of husband, now of manager or friend, enemy or lover. Instead of one mainland there are a thousand islands, each with its own king, and I become a multitude, a poorly organized debating society, without a chairman or an agenda. Moving from island to island, a new "I" is called into being and what was once true now becomes false, what was good becomes bad. The account we give in scuttlebutt and scandal of our encounter with the boss is modified according to whether we tell it to this person or that, according to whether we are acting out this role or that. The peregrination around the islands drags in its wake the burden of hypocrisy, guilt, remorse, and self-hatred.

All the while beneath the surface is the ground swell of the ceaseless alternation between me-as-*center* and me-as-*periphery*. This pull generates anxiety and sometimes dread as the viewpoint becomes astigmatic through the distortions of consciousness dependent upon ill-fitting words, and the center becomes unstable and erratic, forever eluding the verbal net. And so life becomes more restless than a turbulent ocean. Increasingly we seek the one center amid the chaos and so increasingly we become "egotistic," and increasingly we generate conflict with others. Our revitalizing conversations become fewer and the interminable monologue instead causes a never-ending exhaustion of our vital energies. From morning to night there is an endless flow of chatter streaming through the core of consciousness, sometimes made public when we can find a victim, but otherwise continuing in private.

That I am a conversation becomes obvious if I allow my attention, but for a few moments, to dwell upon this, its degenerate form, the internal monologue. This monologue consistently circles about "I" in interminable debates, arguments, lectures, admonishments bestowed upon some unknown recipient hidden somewhere in the shadows of my mind. When this monologue is externalized my victim suffers the fate of the recipient in the shadows and to the tune of blandishments, innuendo, and carefully veiled threats is lured into the gyrations around "I." The cocktail party is the arena par excellence where "I" is the theme of unending variations repeated with relish. Some even acquire a slight stammer when using the word "I" so that they can get two or three shots in for the price of one.

As an experiment go for a day without using the word "I." It will be a day that will drag on forever. If you have given up smoking or some other addiction, you will know the feeling. One's ability to talk with others dries up, and the ability to think clearly suffers. The peaks and valleys of experience seem flattened out and there seems to be "nothing to look forward to."

In the last chapter we spoke of the importance of the center and gave some account of Renée's experience when she lost the center and suffered the horror of the self devouring the self. What she has to say about words and names is also illustrative of the power of the center and its relationship with words. She talks of existence as a country where "reigned an implacable light, blinding, leaving no places for shadow; an immense space without boundary, limitless, flat; a mineral, lunar country, cold as the wastes of the North Pole. In this stretching emptiness all is unchangeable, congealed, crystallized."[31] A world without peaks or valleys, light and shadow, here and there, now and then, a world without center. Renée says, "When I looked at a chair or a jug, I thought not of their use or function, but as having lost their names, their function, and their meaning."[32] Because there was no center, there was no meaning; things did not point beyond themselves but turned in on themselves. This destroyed their relationship, function, and value, while their names became labels which could slip off and reveal things as "things." Renée said, "They became 'things' and began to take on life, to exist."[33] Instead of eye meeting eye in a hostile embrace, as the divided viewpoint struggles to find its inherent unity, eye meets living, tense object and the vortex swings. "I attempted to escape their hold by calling out their names, I said, 'chair, jug, table, it is a table.'"[34] What magician is there who does not know that to control the devil one needs but name the devil. But first the magic circle of which one is the center must be drawn. Without this, one has no power to enchant: "But the words echoed hollowly, deprived of all meaning; it had left the object, was divorced from it so much so that on the one hand it was a living, mocking thing, on the other hand, a name robbed of sense, an envelope emptied of content. Nor was I able to bring the two together, but stood there rooted before them, filled with fear and impotence."[35]

"I" and "it"—twin mountain peaks whose valley is an abyss. "I" and "It," the former *being* the center, the second the center that is *known*. These two lead to the search for power and action on the one hand and certainty and knowledge on the other, and together give rise to the "world as Will and Idea." Some seek leadership to dominate others by *being* that to which they must look for the ultimate decision, the ultimate judgment. "I am, none else beside me." I must be the world's unique and only center. Others seek to *know* "it" as the center. By knowing "it," the bondage of ambiguity is broken and certainty attained. The name of "it" is legion and endless. "It" is all that mankind has sought to know. Each has his own "it" around which the world revolves, each has his own subordinating idea.

Being, reality, matter, atoms, quarks, singularities—"it" is somewhere, that center of all, that immovable ground upon which all is founded. Some believe that the center will be found in knowing how it all began, others in how it will all end. Some physicists believe that it will end at the center of a black hole. A black hole, it is said, is the result of a celestial body collapsing into its own center, and at the center of this center is a "singularity," "a point that might be infinitely, fantastically small, a theoretical edge of space and time. Toward that edge, that minuscule point, races at unimaginable speed all the matter sucked into the black hole, all the matter of a star or even of a universe, to be crushed into a region of infinite density."[36] What a description of the power of Oneness! The Big Bang, from which it all started, also came from a center, one that "was at first no bigger than the proverbial head of a pin. . . . We're not sure whether it came from absolute zero size, but we know that it must have been very small indeed."[37] And through a hole that size we must get not only the universe, but the tail of the ox as well.

The love affair that mankind has had with "it," the center of the universe of words and names, is unending. One such lover was Bertrand Russell.

"Mathematics," said Russell, "takes us from what is human, into the region of absolute necessity, to which not only the actual world, but every possible world, must conform; and here it builds a habitation, or rather finds a habitation eternally standing, where our ideals are fully satisfied and our best hopes are not thwarted. It is only when we thoroughly understand the entire independence of ourselves, which belongs to this world that reason finds, that we can adequately realize the profound importance of its beauty."[38]

This habitation eternally standing, this house of absolute necessity and beauty, is it not Shangri-La? It is the same eternal habitation independent of ourselves that the Catholic philosophers built, or found, in the twelfth and thirteenth centuries, when led by St. Thomas Aquinas and using words as bricks and logic as mortar, they built the imperishable structure of Catholicism to bring heaven down to earth. St. Thomas and Russell—both disciples of the master architect Aristotle, to whose teaching it has been said one must be converted before being able to penetrate the inner sanctum of the Church.

The keystone of Russell's and Aquinas's architecture is what Russell calls a term, which is "anything that can be thought of as one," an undivided unity: apple, house, finger, tail are all examples of what is called a term. Every term, says Russell, is indestructible, immutable, and therefore eternal and unchanging. This is it, this is what we have been looking for: the pinnacle of our conceptual hierarchy, the keystone of our triumphal arch is the term, which can be given the simplest of all names: "A." Its immutability, indestructibility can be expressed in that most self-evident but nonetheless elegant formulation: A = A, the law of identity. The ball has stopped rolling, we are home as last.

But wait! Did we find this keystone, or did we build it? Russell says that mathematics *builds* or *finds* a habitation. On the face of it, it seems such a small point, almost a literary stammer, and he stamps on the worm of doubt when he says that the habitation is entirely independent of ourselves. "It," he says, is quite separate from "I," and herein lies its beauty. This may be so, but did I build it, in which case it is subordinate to "I"; or did

I find it, so that I can be subordinate to it? There is a difference between finding God and creating God. A = A—is it found or created? If it is created, can it be eternal, immutable? Has the tail gotten stuck again?

"Nothing is identical with itself," said Nagarjuna.[39] "One cannot step into the same river twice," said Heraclitus. "Everything is true, nothing is true; everything is both true and not true; everything is neither true nor not true. This is the teaching of the Buddha."[40] High is not high, low is not low. It is said in Zen that a tail is not a tail, that is why it is called a tail. There is a saying: Before I started practicing Zen, mountains were mountains, trees were trees. After I had made some progress, mountains were no longer mountains, trees were no longer trees. But now mountains are again mountains, trees are again trees. A does not equal A, that is why it is called A, and therefore why it can equal A.

Intuition is one thing, its expression is something else, but the struggle must go on, the struggle for the intuition of Oneness to be expressed as "it." The flag, the cause, the ideal, the eternal habitation, the thousand-year Reich—we must find it or build it or we'll never find rest. The flag is the symbol of identity, with it I find myself and it at the center. "A" no less is the symbol of identity, and in the ambiguity of identity lies the heart of the matter. To get this identity, this One, we must get rid of, eliminate, discard, scrape away all that is not it. But strive as we may for the unadulterated, unmixed racial or intellectual purity, we just can't make it. We can get the head, the horns, even all four feet and body through, but damn it, the tail gets stuck! And only the very tip of the tail at that.

One Reich, one Volk, one Führer, one "I." The Reich was one because everything that was not the Reich was smashed, bombed, blasted out of existence. The Volk was one because all who were not the Volk were hanged, gassed, shot, or enslaved. But however pure the blood, it is still red.

And "I"?

A Yorkshireman said, "All the world's a bit queer, except thee and me, and sometimes I'm not so sure about thee."

The ox bellows, "Throughout heaven and earth, I alone am the Honored One," and the hills echo back, "I am, none else beside me." However faintly, the echo goes on reverberating, so powerful is the ox.

"There is no beginning to practice nor end to enlightenment; no beginning to enlightenment or end to practice."

> Someone asked a master, "What is a drop of water from the source of life?"
> "A drop of water from the source of life." [41]

It is not a question of pouring the drop back into the river, nor the river back into the drop. The One must eternally perish in the search for the One.

> Layman P'ang asked Ma-tzu, "Who is the man who doesn't accompany the ten thousand dharmas?"
> (What is Oneness?)
> "I'll tell you after you have swallowed in one swig all the waters of the West River." [42]

A number of blindmen were investigating an ox: one felt its leg and said it was like the branch of a tree; another felt its stomach and said it was round like a barrel; another felt its tail and said it was long like a rope. One with eyes who could see it was an ox laughed and said, "You are all wrong." But was he not the blindest of all?

Sometimes there is no ox, sometimes there is an ox. Sometimes there is an ox and a tail and sometimes Swish! Swish!

It is not a question of letting the tail fade away, become merged, dropping off, or even seeing into it.

> In the absolute moment, the waving of a finger perfects what all the spiritual disciplines can achieve.
>
> If one would follow this way, how much effort one must put in. [43]

8

Who Can We Turn to for Help?

*Tokusan went one night to Ryutan to ask for his
teaching, and stayed until night fell. (After much discussion) Ryutan said, "It is getting late, you had better return." Tokusan made his bows, lifted the blind,
and went out. Seeing that it was dark, he turned back
and said, "It's dark outside." Ryutan thereupon lit a
candle and handed it to him. As Tokusan was about
to take it, Ryutan blew it out. At this Tokusan was
suddenly awakened. He made obeisance. "What have
you realized?" asked Ryutan. Tokusan replied, "From
now on I will not doubt the sayings of any of the
great Zen masters in the world."*

*The next day Ryutan ascended the rostrum and de-
clared, "Among you there is a fellow whose fangs are
like swords and whose mouth is like a bowl of blood.
Strike him with a stick and he won't turn his head to
look at you. One day he will climb to the highest of all
peaks and establish his Way there."*

*Tokusan then made a bonfire of his notes and com-
mentaries on the Diamond Sutra in front of the main
monastery hall and declared, "Even though one masters various profound teachings, it is like placing a
single hair in vast space. Even if one gains all the essential knowledge in the world, it is like throwing a
drop of water into a deep ravine." Having burnt up*

*all his notes and commentaries, he left with grati-
tude.*[1]

Tokusan was a student of the Diamond Sutra, one of the
more important sutras of Zen Buddhism. It is said that he
became very incensed when he heard that the Zen
school talked about people achieving Buddhahood in
this life, as his understanding had led him to believe that
it required innumerable lifetimes to achieve
Buddhahood. He therefore set out to visit some Zen
masters to refute their claim. He carried with him two
basket-loads of commentaries on the Diamond Sutra.

To go off in this way to refute single-handedly a school
of teaching was quite an undertaking and suggests
considerable energy, determination, and certainty on
the part of Tokusan. He had no doubt that he was in the
right and that the Zen teachers were wrong, nor did he
have any doubt that he could set the wrong right.

On his way Tokusan came into collision with an old
woman. This kind of collision with an old woman well
versed in Zen seemed to be an occupational hazard of
itinerant Zen monks, and not infrequently one finds
these scourges appearing to beat the backs of the
mighty. There was even one who tangled with Joshu and
who did not fare too badly in the encounter. The old
woman asked Tokusan a very simple question and it
completely capsized him and his two baskets of
commentaries.

He had stopped at a teahouse run by the old woman
to get some tea and refreshments. The little cakes that

were served were called in Chinese "mind refreshers." She asked Tokusan what he had in his baskets. Tokusan replied, probably with some condescension (he had come to do battle with battleships, not an old tugboat) that he had the Diamond Sutra and a lot of commentaries. Then he probably turned away, waiting for his tea and mind refreshers. "Oh!" said the old woman, "really! Well, let me please ask you a question, and if you can answer it you may have your mind refreshers free. If not, I'm afraid you'll have to go on your way." No doubt with a sort of incredulous smile, Tokusan agreed, wondering what question she could possibly ask and wanting to get on with his tea and cakes. "In the Diamond Sutra it says, 'It is impossible to retain past mind, impossible to hold to present mind, and impossible to grasp future mind.' Pray tell me which mind is your honor wishing to refresh?"

This completely sank Tokusan, and the fact that the knockout came from an old tugboat added insult to injury. This is just like the old lady who insisted that Gutei say a word of Zen before she would consent to take some refreshment with him. Tokusan's old lady is asking for a word of Zen. Tokusan had two basket-loads of words that he had carried hundreds of miles, and not one of them a word of Zen.

The Diamond Sutra is a record of Buddha's teaching, and it is one of the sutras particularly favored by Zen masters. It consists of a series of questions by Subhuti, a close disciple of Buddha, and the responses given by Buddha, which themselves are often in the form of a question. One of the questions that Subhuti asks is, "When people ask 'What is the Way?' how shall we reply? How are we to quiet their drifting minds and subdue their craving thoughts?" Buddha says he will teach the Way to liberate all the innumerable beings, and the Diamond Sutra is the result. In this sutra, one of the questions Buddha asks Subhuti is, "What do you think, has the Buddha a teaching to teach?" And Subhuti says, "No." How are we going to understand this contradiction? On the one hand Buddha says he is going to give a teaching, on the other he says he does not give a teaching. If we can understand this, we can understand why Ryutan blew out the candle Tokusan was holding and also what is in the mind of a teacher who is worth obeying.

All of human knowledge is concerned with the *content* of mind. Even physics and chemistry are concerned with the content of mind. Zen is concerned with *mind itself.* There is a saying: "Stone, no dog: dog, no stone." On the face of it there is a yapping dog and someone searching for a stone to fling at it. But there is another meaning altogether. If you have a stone dog, you can look at the shape and kind of dog, how well or how poorly the artist has captured the likeness, and so on. In this case the stone is not noticed. Or alternatively, you can admire the stone, the smoothness, the color, and so on. In this case the dog is not noticed.

The *form* of the dog makes it something particular and definite. It is there, you can touch it, give it a name. The stone *relative* to the form could be said to be infinite. No matter how many stone dogs there are, there is still stone left over. There can be stone horses, cows, pigs, as well as dogs. Stone is ubiquitous as well as infinite. Furthermore, the form the stone takes does not give any information about the stone itself.

In much the same way there is mind and form (content) of mind. Mind is comparable to stone; the content of mind is comparable to the form the stone takes. Zen, it might be said, is concerned with the stone. However, stone always comes in some form, even if the form is simply a lump. So Zen cannot ignore the form.

The form that mind has is trees and houses, cars and

buses, people and cats, sunshine and rain. The contours of this mindscape are etched by words and thoughts, by formulae and systems. If we could see the mind as a lump, it would be a lump of knowing/being.

The "stone" of the mind, the philosopher's stone, is Oneness. "One I seek. One I know, One I see, One I call." Mind is One mind, just as the dog is a stone dog. If there is no stone there is no dog. If there is no One mind there is no perception and sensation, thought and language.

The transition from One mind to trees and names, houses and systems, stars and formulae, food and menus is "idea." Idea focuses "One mind" and this focus is called attention. There is no fundamental difference between One mind, idea, and attention, just as there is no fundamental difference between a quarry, a rock in the quarry, and a pebble in the rock. We always give attention to things, but things owe their thinghood to idea; in substance they are One mind. The substance of all substance is One mind.

The fundamental idea is "I am" and fundamental to all life, from amoeba to man, is the idea "given that I am." One might say that this is the experience of the "instinct to survive." On the other hand, the basis for attention is "it is." "I am" and "it is" are pivoted around the central point and the uneasy balance gives rise to the question "Who am I and what is it?"

Culture and civilization are in a way the graveyards of the struggle between one and the other, "I" and "it," for supremacy: "Who am I?" "What is it?" Idea after idea has been generated to quell the struggle and to bring a measure of peace and order, and each in turn has succumbed to the ossification of language. As each idea comes into being it becomes a thing identified and fixed through the medium of attention and words.

Each idea, as the emissary of Oneness, has its own center, and is at the same time one of a constellation of ideas that gravitates around one or more other ideas. Each idea plays the role of sun or planet in a galaxy of ideas. The idea "tree" is the center for the ideas "branch," "leaf," "trunk," "root." But it also swings around and draws strength from ideas such as Christmas (tree), Bo (tree), family (tree).

When the center of an idea is "charged," the idea is aroused, and this charge comes from central ideas deeply embedded in the mind; when an idea is charged its satellites are also lit up as a consequence. Each cluster of ideas is therefore related to all other clusters and a hierarchy of ideas is created, all of which make up what is called the conscious mind. At the very center and pinnacle is "I am" and "it is."

This hierarchy of ideas is also a hierarchy of value and of what is important, as well as of certainty and reality. The nearer to the center an idea finds itself, the greater the importance and value of the idea. "Old Glory," "Super Bowl," "Uncle Sam" are much more important and real to an American than to an Englishman, for whom the "Union Jack," "Wimbledon," and "John Bull" are more important and real.

Each situation evokes its own train of ideas, and situations which are often repeated evoke a familiar train. A new situation can cause an upheaval in the distribution of ideas and in their hierarchy. The mind is justly compared to an ocean, which is sometimes calm, sometimes swaying with a slight swell, and at other times torn and blustering in a gale. Remaining in a hermitage where all is constant, repetitive, and expected can bring about a calm and placidity allowing the waves to die down and the ocean to become clear and lucid. But alas, the slightest breeze and the calm is ruffled once more.

Psychotherapy reorganizes the distribution of ideas, sets up new hierarchies, and breaks up clusters of ideas that are welded around traumatic events. But no matter how much order is brought about in this way, true peace of mind will not come because the order is related to a central unique idea, "I am" or "it is," one but also two, riding unsteadily on the horns of the fundamental ambiguity.

When the Buddha says he has no teaching he means that he has no formula to help in the restructuring of the hierarchy. He has no new Weltanschauung to offer, no new codifying ideology which will make sense of it all, give new meaning, a new point to life. Instead he goes directly to the swirling ocean of birth and death, of "now this and now that," those vain attempts at finding true rest. He transcends this ocean just as the one who sees the stone but no dog transcends the world of form.

This swirling ocean, for all its bitterness and brine, is precious to us because it is our conscious world, our world of light. Each idea is like a candle lighting up what we feel is the dark cavern of ignorance. "I am the light of the world," said Christ, and people have misunderstood and taken it that Christ was advertising himself as some high-powered candle which would burn forever. Christ is indeed the light, the sun of the world, but as the alchemist says, "Our sun is a black sun."

> Lead kindly light amid the encircling gloom
> Lead thou me on.
> The night is dark and I am far from home,
> Lead thou me on.

Thus sings the lovely Christian hymn. But what happens if the light goes out, if all the lights go out? Do we continue to see? Buddha asks in the Surangama Sutra, "If the bell stops ringing, do you stop hearing?" If all the ideas are stopped and transcended, do you stop knowing?

Some people teach that fundamentally the mind is a not-knowing mind. Ah, what a pity that such a teaching is taught when mind is knowing itself, knowing/being. Others teach that "I and it" must be welded together, the two opposing horns snapped shut. First dam up a person's capacity to generate new ideas and thought and then fix a center midst a few slogans having the appearance of profundity, but which are in effect mind-boggling nonsense: "If you don't get it, you ain't got it,"[2] or some such phrase repeated ad nauseam. Unfortunately, some of these ways draw upon Zen as an authority for support since there is a superficial resemblance to Zen. It is important to see the difference.

> Thinking to a cult member is just like being stabbed in the heart with a dagger. It is very painful because they've been told that the mind is Satan and thinking is the machinery of the devil. When you deprogram people, you force them to think.[3]

> "Thinking," said an est student, "is the enemy."[4]

> "Words (and therefore thoughts) are of the devil," said a Zen master.

> "Almost every major cult and group teaches some form of not-thinking," said a cult researcher.

> "Cut off all useless thoughts and words and there's nowhere you cannot go," said the Third Patriarch.

If one reads the verses of *Affirming Faith in Mind by the Third Patriarch* (from which the two lines quoted above are taken), it is evident that it is the judgments that underlie the useless thoughts and words that are the target. The verses begin with the following two lines:

> The great Way is not difficult

For those who have no preferences.

These preferences are based upon judgments of value which derive their strength from the center and their energy from the struggle of "*I* am" with "it is." It is precisely by these judgments that the complex architecture of the mind is set up and maintained around one or another center. We try to establish an absolute center, we try to claim some ultimate value or certainty to rest from the swirling undulations of our everyday mind of hassles and frustration. It is like a man at sea slaking his thirst momentarily by drinking salt water. Even as the value or certainty seems most eternal, it is undermined by its very one-sidedness and the mad dance starts all over again. The foundations of "our eternal habitation" are shattered once more. And so a new judgment, a new center is called for.

The Third Patriarch, along with all other Zen masters, is saying, don't be deceived: transcend your struggle for that eternal center; suffer the ambiguities, dilemmas, and complexities of everyday life; search in these and you will find what you seek. "Arouse the mind," says the Diamond Sutra, "without resting it on anything." This certainty that we protect so ferociously, this value that we prize over life itself, are but candles—a brief puff of wind and their flame is gone. The Third Patriarch does not say: kill the mind, do not arouse the mind. He does not say: stop the yearning for Oneness.

A Zen master, Wo-lun, is reported to have been very pleased with his ability to cut off all thoughts, so much so that he composed the following:

> Wo-lun possesses a special aptitude
> He can cut off all thoughts.
> No situation can stir his mind
> The Bodhi-tree grows daily in him.[5]

Hui-neng, the great Zen patriarch, realized the danger that such teaching might generate and composed the following reply:

> Hui-neng has no special aptitude
> He does not cut off any thoughts.
> His mind responds to all situations.
> In what way can the Bodhi-tree grow?[6]

To stop thinking in Zen is to go beyond thinking; that is, to go beyond the need for a point of absolute rest, of absolute truth, goodness, or reality, which is inevitably centered in an ego or some object in the "real" world. In this way the mind finds freedom. Fundamental to Buddhist teaching is "no *I* am," "no *it* is," and "no permanent real world." But also fundamentally it is the Buddha's teaching that all must see into these truths for themselves. This is so different from the cult that says, "What is inside your mind is lies. We are your mind. The Group is your mind."

A cult member, reporting on his emergence from the trance of death induced by a cult, said, "My mind was working for the first time. . . . It didn't want to go back to not thinking again (but) I had a horrible dread that this was *it*—I had sinned and now I would pay the price, . . . become possessed, insane, and all the other things the Church had convinced me would happen if I lost God."

Hui-neng said, "Those who cling to the void vilify the Scriptures by saying they have no use for words and letters. But anyone who says he has no use for words and letters contradicts himself by his very speech because this too is a form of words and letters."

Against those who cling literally to "no setting up of words and letters," Hui-neng said, "Even this phrase 'no words and letters' belongs to words and letters. As soon as they see someone expound the Dharma they would immediately jump upon him as one attached to the use of words and letters! You should know that such people are not only deluded in themselves, but are actually disparaging the Scriptures."[7]

It is not in destroying the ambiguity that peace lies. To clog the ambiguity, muffle or snap it, is like breaking a bow: the archer will never fire another arrow. It is precisely this tension that gives the mind its resilience. When the tension is snapped, great joy and energy may be released in a flood of relief. But within a shorter or longer period of time the joy goes, the energy dries up, and the person collapses into listlessness and disinterest.

A Zen master said that a Zen teacher (actually he said this of a Zen koan, but where is the difference between a teacher and a koan?) is someone who, meeting a blind man groping hesitantly along the edge of a precipice, tapping gingerly with his cane, seizes the cane and throws it away, turns the blind man around thrice and goes away and leaves him.

Or he simply blows out the student's candle.

After Tokusan had his encounter with the old lady, he must have felt very much like a blind man on the edge of a cliff, and Ryutan must have seen this when they met. It is said that the two spent the evening together, but it is not likely that they would have spent much time in small talk. Tokusan was a desperate man. He had sailed for years on the ocean of birth and death with the Diamond Sutra and he knew every plank, spar, and rope, and he had two baskets of notes to prove it. It was his sutra, but with one little bump an old dilapidated tug had capsized him and he was up to his ears in the bitter brine of confusion.

The chances are that he tried to justify his position to Ryutan, perhaps disparaging the old lady a bit, commenting perhaps on how people ask stupid questions, and at the same time trying this answer, that answer, this the same time trying this answer, that answer, this quote, that quote—wanting to smother the voice which would not be smothered.

Perhaps Ryutan answered him, perhaps he didn't. It would not have made any difference either way. It was enough that he was there. It's like "dokusan" (private encounter one has with one's teacher): if you don't know what you are talking about, it's as though the teacher were a wall a hundred feet high; if you do, it's as though there is just vast empty space.

Eventually Tokusan had to leave. Can you imagine the dread he must have felt. When he looked out, it was not only the night that was dark, but also his soul. All that he prized and valued was shattered and in ruins around him, split open by a stupid old woman who knows no better than to serve tea and ask idiotic questions. One last surge of pride, one glimmer of uniqueness, of light, of security. A single candle! Not much, flickering, uncertain, but enough to lighten the darkness. And then, Poof!

The confusion that surrounds "not thinking" is intimately connected to another equally serious confusion: the confusion surrounding the teacher. And one of the questions that lies in the background, so to speak, of this koan is: "What is the function of a teacher?" and its corollary: "What is the function of the student?" To put it in the context of this koan: "What right has Ryutan to blow out Tokusan's candle?"

Yun-men went seeking teaching from Zen master Mu-chou. For three days he stood knocking at the master's door and for three days the master periodically opened the door, gave him a quick look, and then slammed the door. Finally, when the master came for his periodic peek, as soon as the door was open Yun-men squeezed himself in. The master seized him, yelling "Speak, speak!" Yun-men fumbled for something to say.

The master threw him out, calling him useless and slamming the door so hard on Yun-men's leg that he broke it. Yun-men was at this moment awakened.

Gutei cut off his student's finger. Rinzai's teacher struck him each time he asked a question, and Rinzai himself was famous for his shouts and his blows.

> When the Shang-tso Ting came to see Rinzai he asked, "What is the cardinal principle of the Buddha-dharma?" The master got down from his rope-bottomed chair. Seizing the Shang-tso, he gave him a slap and pushed him away. The Shang-tso stood still. A monk standing by said, "Shang-tso Ting, why don't you bow?" Just as he bowed, the Shang-tso came to great awakening.[8]

Shang-tso Ting also doesn't understand: you might say he's blown out of his mind, but still he bows. Why does he bow? Someone said, "You know, if a Zen master hit me, I'd hit him back." Of course, that is why we practice Zen, and must go on practicing Zen until we too bow when we are struck and do not even have the inclination to strike back. "But," this person protested, "is your teacher God then? Does he know you so well that he knows just when to hit and when not to hit? Can he not make a mistake? If you don't strike back, surely you have a right to complain?" Well, . . .

Let it be said before there is any misunderstanding that my teacher has never physically struck me or anyone else, nor has he ever verbally abused or insulted anyone, or even raised his voice in real or simulated anger. He has, however, said things which are extremely painful, sometimes harshly critical; sometimes, it seemed, unnecessarily so. How should one behave toward a teacher who does this?

Another question which my interlocutor would always get very exercised about is obedience. "Do you

mean to tell me that you have to obey your teacher? That
is too much. It might be OK for the Japanese and
Chinese, but for the Westerner, and above all for the
American, this just won't wash. It has taken us all our
time to become free men, why chuck all that striving
away and become a spiritual yes man? Isn't freedom
what Zen is all about? Why all the conformity then?"

The difficulties of the Way are such that very few
people are capable of negotiating the shoals and reefs
alone. Even with a teacher there is no guarantee of
success and without a teacher the seeker is almost
certain to end up circling around and around a point,
unable to advance or retreat.

Spiritual work calls for sacrifice. "Sell all you have and
give to the poor," was Christ's injunction. Obedience
calls for the supreme sacrifice. It calls for the sacrifice of
one's pride, one's *uniqueness*. To obey is to sacrifice
one's center. Robert Burns prayed that some power
would give us the gift to see ourselves as others see us.
How many of us could stand the shock—to find ourselves
suddenly and literally one among millions, to lose in a
moment the precious sense of uniqueness which gives
value and meaning to everything we touch?

And yet, are we "more" unique than our brother? The
question makes no sense grammatically nor in reality. If
we could see ourselves as others see us, or better still,
see others as they see themselves, would we not lay the
demon to rest that leads us like a bull to perpetual
slaughter? Would we not in that moment of undifferen-
tiated vision see all as One? But what a sacrifice that
would be.

In Mexico there are some caves several miles long. In
the caves there are precipitous drops and blind alleys.
There is no electric light, one goes by candlelight only,
led by a guide one has never met before. All the time
there is the question: What if the candle is blown out?

What if the guide blows out the candle? To follow a teacher calls for great faith at times when the capacity for faith is weakest. Exploring the dark labyrinth of the mind, disturbing old ghosts, crossing forbidden thresholds, the seeker sometimes has only the teacher's word that all is well. "Let go of your hold on the cliff!" "Sell all you have and follow me." Sacrifice all to gain all.

But what is this sacrifice? Is it simply a lopping off, a blowing out, a destruction? Or is it perhaps a surrender, a giving up to the teacher, a variation of the famous "transference" of psychoanalysis,[9] transferring through love or hate the unique center from oneself to the teacher; dying as oneself and being resurrected as the Guru?

Of all the repositories for the unique center, none is as perfect as the religious leader—the one who can awaken our numinous yearning for Oneness. The tree, the cross, the icon—these are but surrogates. The teacher is alive, breathing and talking. Is it not his function to herald this yearning and to awaken it? Is there a power greater than the human voice to do this for us? To read a truth is one thing, but as the politician no less than the evangelist knows so well, to hear it spoken is quite something else. What is more natural than for a disciple to conceive that because a teacher is the source of the awakening of this yearning for Oneness, he or she will at the same time be the object which can satisfy that yearning.

The problem is that many teachers believe that they are worthy of this kind of adoration that their disciples are projecting. Often what makes a person assume the role of a teacher is the arousal of Oneness within through an enlightenment, a samadhi, or even an awakening. The effect of this encounter with, or as, Oneness is often inflation, the newly awakened one feeling that he has become privy to some great secret which he takes it upon himself to deliver to mankind, who should therefore be duly grateful.

Hakuin, one of the greatest Zen masters, tells of his own awakening after strenuously working on the koan Mu. He had been working day and night without eating or resting when suddenly a great doubt manifested itself in him. He said it was as though he were frozen solid in a sheet of ice extending tens of thousands of miles. His breast seemed filled with purity and he could go neither forward not backward. "To all intents and purposes I was out of my mind and Mu alone remained." This state of samadhi, he said, lasted for several days. Then he chanced to hear the sound of the temple bell and was suddenly transformed. It was as though a sheet of ice had been cracked or a jade tower had fallen with a crash. Suddenly he returned to his senses. All his doubts were gone and in a loud voice he called, "Wonder of wonders, there is no cycle of birth and death through which one must pass, there is no awakening one must seek." Then—what many people will find surprising—Hakuin said, "My pride soared up like a majestic mountain; my arrogance surged forward like the tide." Simply I thought to myself, "In the past two or three hundred years, no one could have accomplished such a marvelous break-through as this."[10]

It is useful to compare what Hakuin and Tokusan have to say at the end of the koan quoted above, and see that they both speak very expansively and one-sidedly. A good teacher will have prepared the student for the likelihood of the arising of this inflation and will have warned that awakening is but the beginning of practice and not its end. Kapleau-roshi repeats this again and again, as did his teacher Yasutani-roshi. Hakuin went off to see a master about his awakening, or, as he said, "Shouldering my glorious enlightenment, I set out at once for Shinano." Fortunately for Hakuin, the Zen master was onto him and started calling Hakuin a poor devil in the hole as soon as he saw him, and gave him another koan to work on.

"One evening the master sat cooling himself on the verandah. Again I brought him a verse I had written. 'Delusion and fancies,' the master said. I shouted his words back at him in a loud voice, whereupon the master seized me and rained twenty or thirty blows with his fist on me, and then pushed me off the verandah. I lay stretched out in the mud as though dead, scarcely breathing and almost unconscious. I could not move; meanwhile the master sat on the verandah roaring with laughter. After a short while I regained consciousness, got up, and bowed to the master. My body was bathed in perspiration. The master called out to me in a loud voice, 'You poor devil in the hole!'[11]

Suppose Hakuin had not gone to see Shoju, or that there had been no tradition of Zen masters sanctioning the awakening of their students. With Shoju, Hakuin gained deeper awakening yet, seeing through his own inflation. But had he not done so, had he instead set up his dojo, zendo, ashram, or whatever after his first awakening, what devastation he would have wreaked upon his unwitting followers. Hakuin's encounter with Shoju was undoubtedly a major turning point in his spiritual life, and it laid the foundation for all that followed. Shoju saw Hakuin's inflation, and that he was about to invest his uniqueness in the numinous oneness that arises with awakening—a spiritually devastating mixture—consequently humiliating Hakuin was the greatest compassion. Humiliation is the most painful of all medicines and the most dangerous. Suppose Shoju had not been a great teacher and Hakuin had not been a student with the heart of a lion, then what? Or worse still, suppose Shoju had encouraged Hakuin in his exaltation. Suppose Shoju had fed Hakuin the poison that says exaltation, being blissed out, or being ecstatic is what it's all about. Supposing Nansen had replied to Joshu's question, "What is the Way?" by saying "Getting real high!"

A woman who had an encounter with the growth movement est said, "It was beautiful. I was out of touch with reality; it was as though I could see on a different dimension. I experienced an intense joy all the time. I reached a point where fantasies became real. It was poetical. I was speaking in biblical languages. At times I couldn't open my mouth, but when I did it came out in verse. I was alone in my apartment for a week and I felt like I was getting a new body, a renewal. I was extremely active. I couldn't stop dancing. I didn't want to stop, it was so good. My body felt so powerful."[12] She ended in a psychiatric ward and spent the next year sorting herself out.

One of the ways to help a person struggle with uniqueness and its attendant pride is to insist upon obedience. For example, pride has always been the major sin for Christians and obedience is one of the vows which, along with chastity and poverty, a monk or nun takes. St. Ignatius puts this as a primary rule:

> Putting aside all private judgments, we should keep our minds prepared and ready to obey promptly and in all the . . . church.[13]

The ego—that unholy alliance of center, uniqueness, and language—is a rock upon which spiritual aspiration founders. Until this alliance is broken up and each freed to find its own place in the ecology of the ebb and flow of life, it will simply break up each fresh stream of hope. But the rock is hard and has endured the worst of the weather of experience. Spiritual obedience, surrendering to a higher authority, is painful and confusing, but it is dynamite. The three vows of obedience, poverty, and chastity are designed, each in its own way, to unseat the tyranny of "I am."

But is obedience just obedience?

> The only kind of obedience that effectively shapes our character is obedience performed against our will and our own ideas. . . . In true obedience you obey without seeing the reason for what you are told to do, and in spite of your own reluctance. A special blessing is promised for such obedience.[14]

This was said by Theophan the Recluse, a profoundly religious man.

> We were all so trained to obey orders without thinking that the thought of disobeying an order would simply never have occurred to anyone. . . . I did not reflect on it at the time. I had been given an order.[15]

This was said by Hess, commandant of Auschwitz. The order he had given was to exterminate millions of human beings.

A famous experiment on obedience and authority was reported on thus:

> The experiment I set up was relatively simple: a person comes to the laboratory and, in the context of a learning experiment, he is told to give increasingly severe electric shocks to another person (who, unknown to the subject, is a confederate and does not actually receive the shocks). This arrangement gave me a chance to see how far people would go before they refused to follow the experimenter's orders. . . . Many subjects obeyed the experimenter no matter how vehement the pleading of the person being

shocked, no matter how painful the shocks seemed to be and no matter how much the victim pleaded to be let out. This was seen time and again in our studies and has been observed in several universities.[16]

"If my heart and your teaching disagree, what should I do?" "They cannot disagree," said the teacher. "Yes, they can and they do," he said. "Then you should follow my teaching."

An ex-Zen monk has set himself up as a counselor for people who wish, but are unable, to leave spiritual groups. These people have become so dependent upon the spiritual group that they are unable to face life without it, but so disenchanted by the teaching that they are unable to face life with it.

Buddha said, "Hold fast to the truth as a lamp. Seek salvation alone in the truth. Look not for assistance to anyone beside yourself."

How is one to find one's way through this spiritual minefield of obedience? On the one hand we have heroic stories of Milarepa and Naropa obediently and unquestioningly following their teachers' instructions, performing prodigious work along the spiritual path. On the other hand there are stories of people who become totally addicted to their teacher to the point of madness. For centuries spiritual seekers of all religions have been exhorted to obey, even at the risk of their life and sanity. Yet the catastrophe of Nazism could never have occurred but for this very obedience.

An ex-member of a cult writes:

> I used to think that my journey inward was also carrying me toward maturity, that the end of my search would inevitably come with the realization of some universal meaning. I did not ask for Gods, only for a controlling center inside myself. Now instead of

growth and conviction, I find I have acquired an intricate set of rules that define my actions in life's games.[17]

It is in this that the heart of the problem lies. Christ said, "I don't bring peace but a sword," and "Whoever is near me is near the fire," but people do not understand. Kapleau-roshi points out that Zen does not seek to make you comfortable, but strong. "It is not a way out of life's problems, but a way into them." "What is the Way?" asked Joshu. "Everyday life is the Way." Facing everyday life, with its aches and pains, uncertainties and ambiguities. This is the way.

The Russian teacher Gurdjieff always insisted that one should be at least at the level of a good family man or woman to be able to practice his way. If one cannot put up with a wife or husband and a family, if one cannot work with others to the point of being able to earn money to live on, if one isn't able to discipline oneself to maintain a routine for oneself and by oneself, then truly no teacher on earth is going to be able to help. This is not to say that one has to be married, etc., in order to make one's way along the spiritual path, but that one should be at this level. Some spiritual practitioners tend to look down on the householder, feeling this is not compatible with spiritual work. On the contrary, if a person can get his or her life together at this level, there is then some chance the person can get it together on the spiritual level, and will not use spiritual work as just another compensation, something to give life meaning.

Many are called in Christianity, Buddhism, or any other true religion, but few are chosen; not because these religions are elitist, but because some people go to them for the wrong reasons. Christ said, "Pick up your cross and follow me." This is the first thing we must do. But some go to Christ in the hope that he will carry their cross for them or in the belief that he has already done so. Faith in Christ is the faith that no matter how heavy the cross, it will never crush us. People take up the "spiritual path" because they want to be perfect, or because they want certainty, or because they want security. But it is precisely in the sacrifice of perfection, certainty, and security that we walk the path. It is only when we no longer seek peace from obedience that we can become strong by obeying.

The basic ambiguity, as we have said, is resolved by the establishment of a center, and obedience may be one of the ways that the fixed center is established. However, there is no less "ego" involved in belonging to a group than there is in being independent of a group. Submerging me-as-center to a fixed center to which I am periphery—be it the flag, the church, or the pagoda—is its own form of allying uniqueness, center, and language. Self-sacrifice, belonging, obedience—these are then but ways to reinforce the fixed center.

It is a well-known axiom that the one who cannot obey cannot command. Obedience in this instance often means to conform, and conformity is a group require-ment. The leader must conform to the group's image of a leader as well as the follower to the group's image of a follower. Even chicks will peck to death the odd one out. This obedience has a functional value. But this kind of obedience has nothing in common with spiritual obedience. One does not obey a true spiritual teacher to make life easier, nor to ensure the smooth running of a group. The general formula "teacher says" has no place at all in spiritual work because it is simply an invitation to sink into the comfort of "belonging" to a group.

Very often in religious groups the leader is also the head administrator: separation of "church and state" is rarely recognized. Therefore, when a teacher gives an administrative instruction, two kinds of obedience are inextricably bound: spiritual and functional. This can be the source of a great deal of frustration and difficulty. A teacher, for example, might be in the wrong in something that he does as an administrator. However, because it is felt that one must obey the teacher, to point out the error is likely to invite others to judge one as egotistic. But of course, awakening or enlightenment do not make one more intelligent or farseeing as an administrator. On the contrary, genuine awakening is so hard to come by and requires so much application that there is a good chance that the teacher has not had the time to acquire administrative skills.

No teacher is perfect, infallible, or omniscient—all have their failings. Indeed, it might well be because he has so many failings and has struggled so hard to put right as much as he can that he is a good teacher. One can be quite sure that any claim to be perfect is an empty one. The journey we are taking is millions of miles long and the best teacher but a few paces ahead. There will be areas in which one is more competent than the teacher, and to pretend otherwise is to invite trouble.

No teacher worth his or her salt is going to expect students to obey completely and at all times, and a teacher who does not rejoice when he sees a student standing up for something that the student believes is right should surely start looking around for a teacher himself. It is not an act of betrayal to point out where one feels a teacher is mistaken, provided one has the experience and wisdom to see how and when to do it. On the other hand, one should not necessarily expect the teacher to be delighted at being told he is making a mistake or is wrong.

People often look to a teacher to be the unique, stable center of their existence; this is why they pretend the mistakes their teacher sometimes makes display some mysterious wisdom that the ordinary person can never discover. Teachers occasionally do and say foolish things because they are human and one must face up to this even while accepting them as teachers. "Teacher says," "Guruji says" is enough in many spiritual groups to stop all argument. To continue the argument indicates one's "ego, conceit, intransigence," and so on. If what a teacher says does not accord with what one's heart tells one is the case, then we should struggle with the contradiction. Perhaps he is wiser than we are, perhaps he is testing us—or perhaps he is wrong.

If one cannot obey any teacher then the chances are that one cannot obey anyone and this is a kind of sickness. But obedience is not necessarily pleasant—on the contrary, if it is pleasant, if one finds rest and peace in the idea of obedience, then one must beware because this is the way to enslavement. If one finds peace and security in obedience, if one is attracted to a teacher because of his "charisma" more than his teaching, for his "strength" more than his awakening, for his "deep compassion" more than his common sense, then obedience will feed the ego like clover feeds a horse, filling it full of gas.

Obedience is painful because with it one breaks the grip of ego. It doesn't matter whether the teacher is right or wrong, so long as no one is going to get hurt in the process. It doesn't matter whether what the teacher says is just or unjust. This struggle with uniqueness, with the imperative to be always right, first, best, and perfect has no enemies, only allies. How much more of an ally, therefore, is the person who is dedicating his or her life to help you.

9

What Do We Need to Know?

*Once, in ancient times, the World-Honored One came
to the place where many Buddhas were assembled.
When Manjusri arrived there the Buddhas all returned to their original places. A single woman was
there, close to Buddha's throne, in the deepest meditation. Manjusri said to the Buddha, "How is it that this
woman is so close to your throne, and I cannot be?"
The Buddha spoke to Manjusri and said, "You may
awaken this woman from her deep meditation and
ask her yourself how this can be." Manjusri walked
around her three times, snapped his fingers once,
then took her up to the Brahma Heaven and tried all
his supernatural powers, but could not bring her out
of her deep meditation. The World-Honored One said,
"Even a hundred thousand Manjusris could not get
her out of her concentrated condition. But down
below, past one billion, two hundred million countries, as innumerable as the sands of the Ganges,
there is a Bodhisattva named Momyo. He will be able
to awaken this woman from her profound meditation." Thereupon Momyo emerged out of the earth
and bowed to the World-Honored One, who told him
what he wanted him to do. Momyo then walked to
the woman, snapped his fingers once, and at this
she came out of her meditation.[1]*

Manjusri and Momyo, Buddha and the woman, oneness and twoness, the clay and the jug. There are no absolutes because in a way everything is its opposite in disguise. When Gutei's assistant pointed his finger, was it at Buddha or at the woman? And when it was cut off, what did he point to then? What is the Way? Buddha is the Way, the woman is the Way, everyday mind is the Way. What would the woman be without Buddha? But what would Buddha be without the woman?

Why can the woman be close to Buddha while Manjusri cannot? The sutra from which this scene is taken was obviously written before the days of women's liberation—the most a woman could hope for then, if she were good, was to be reborn as a man. This is the background to Manjusri's question. What he means is, why is it that a woman, confused and inferior, can sit next to the Buddha but I cannot?

"Judge not that ye be not judged," said Christ. A Zen verse says, "One judgment and Buddha is a common man. A moment of no judgment and a common man is Buddha." Judgment is the cleaver by which we butcher the life of the world and resurrect it as a kingdom of words and theories of which I am king.

A Zen master said, "As for skin, what a difference (between men and women). As for bones, where's the difference?" How sad it is when women throw away their womanhood crying, "Women are the same as men," and protest that women have no need for men. It is true that women are the same as men; but who wants to live in a world of bones? It is true that women do not need men, but there should be joy, not bitterness, in that "not need," and in being liberated as a human being. High is not high and low is not low; but on a hill, what a wonderful view, and in the valley, what lush meadows.

Everything is different and not even itself for an instant. We cannot step into the same stream twice, nor even repeat our own name. Some say that the mind of differentiation is an obstacle. But to see differences is not wrong. Addiction to the absolute and unchanging, the unique center and static world it creates, this is the error. But on the other hand, everything is One. Everything is the miraculous emanation of One Mind, and the error is to shatter this One Mind as the reflection of the moon is shattered on the restless waves of the sea.

A woman is Buddha as woman; a man is Buddha as man. An ignorant person is Buddha as an ignorant person; a wise person is Buddha as a wise person.

Why can a woman sit close to Buddha, while Manjusri cannot? Why can Momyo awaken her and Manjusri cannot? Why did all the Buddhas return to Buddhaland when Manjusri appeared? In any case, who are Buddha, Manjusri, and Momyo, and what can this ancient scene tell us about the workings of our own mind?

First let us consider the word Buddha. *Who was Buddha?* Was he a kind of Christ, or prophet such as is found in the Old Testament? Was he some kind of God or incarnation? If so, what does it mean when Zen masters affirm that our own mind is Buddha, that all is Buddha?

The word *Buddha,* like other Sanskrit words such as Bodhisattva, Manjusri, and so on, can be understood in four different ways, much as the image of the woman in Figure 1 can be seen in two different ways: as an old/young woman. The four ways, for want of better words, can be called the personal, universal, transcendent, and unique. As a person, Buddha lived and died; each of us meets the universal Buddha face to face when coming to Awakening; the transcendent Buddha is One Mind; the unique Buddha is and has been worshiped by countless millions as the one stable and absolute center.

Buddha, the person who lived and died, was called Siddhartha Gautama and later in his life was also known as Shakyamuni, the saint or wise man of the Shakya tribe. From all accounts, he was born into a wealthy family, the son of a king or tribal chief. He was a very accomplished person and enjoyed a life of privilege and luxury. He was married and had a son. But the time came when he became restless and dissatisfied, and this restlessness led him to realize what most of us come to realize sooner or later: that there is something fundamentally amiss in life. We work, suffer, strive, and labor, trying to get one thing or another accomplished which rarely, if ever, outlives us, and with which in any case we often become bored before it is finished. We are always seeking for some final consummation which constantly eludes us and all the time our life slips away in trivialities; even what we love, respect, and treasure gets worn out, dies, and finally goes away. Sickness, old age, and death stalk us and in the end we die and are seemingly swallowed up in an oblivion of forgetfulness. Everything that we can see, touch, or hear is likewise on its way to oblivion. One day the earth and the sun as well will spin off their axes and plunge into an abyss of forgetfulness, wiping out even the last trace of history, science, and religious belief. Why do we live? What is it all about? What is intelligence? What is life? What is death? What must we do which is worthwhile?

These questions must have tormented Siddhartha Gautama unbearably because he gave up everything—family, friends, power, position—and went off on his own to try to find peace of mind. He did all sorts of things: met a lot of teachers, tried yoga and ascetic practices, but still the nagging questions would not leave him. What is worthwhile? Finally he worked himself into a complete cul-de-sac. Nothing he could do, not even committing suicide, nothing that he could learn, nothing that he could experience or even be conscious of, would solve this problem, because everything was impermanent, everything comes and goes, and that which he sought had to transcend this transience. He had reached the end of the road, but not the end of the journey, and he *had* to go on. He could not possibly find the answer, yet he *had* to find the answer. The answer meant more to him than life itself, but death could not give it.

In this desperate state of mind he sat down in deep meditation, and unmoved by the assaults and seductions of the furies and sirens and regardless of the humiliations and betrayals of the Monarch of Death, broke out of the cul-de-sac and into life.

> O wonder of wonders!
> All life without exception is life without limit.

Shakyamuni was a remarkable man in many ways, but he was not supernatural. Each of us is remarkable in some way or other, but all of us are ordinary people. The President of the United States, the Queen of England, the superstars of sports, films, and music, the saints and sinners are all ordinary people. They eat and sleep, go to the bathroom, get sick; are nice people in some ways, bores in other ways. All are oppressed by the same anxieties and tensions. We often excuse ourselves by saying, "It is all right for that person because he or she is this or that," and forget that they are this and that while being quite ordinary people. It is in his very ordinariness that Buddha is universal and it is in our ordinariness only that we can meet this Buddha face to face.

> This earth where we stand is the Pure Lotus Land,
> This very body the body of Buddha.[2]

The universal Buddha is the one we meet face to face upon awakening.

A sleepy-eyed grandam
Encounters herself in an old mirror.
Clearly she sees a face
But it doesn't resemble her at all.
Too bad, with muddled head
She tries to recognize her reflection.[3]

A Zen master came to awakening on seeing his face reflected in a stream and wrote:

You should not search through others
Lest the truth recede farther from you.
When alone I proceed through myself,
I meet him wherever I go.
He is the same as me.
Yet I am not he!
Only if you understand this
Will you be one with Tathagata (Buddha).[4]

Mumon said, "If you can see him and are absolutely clear about him, it will be like coming upon your own father at the crossroads."[5]

"Throughout heaven and earth, I alone am the Honored One." But the heavens and earth are the Honored One too.

The transcendent Buddha is the Lord of the Aeon, sustaining heaven and earth, counting the stars and galaxies while protecting even the ants that crawl, and loving all that breathes, intimately connected with all, yet nevertheless a resplendent and luminous sun that gives life to the furthest reaches. As aeon succeeds aeon, the Lord of the Aeon radiates luminous intelligence, suffuses all with the cool warmth of the tranquility of compassion, and upholds the greatest and smallest.

All the Buddhas, saviors of the world,

Dwelling in mighty divine penetration
In order to gladden all creatures
Reveal their infinite power divine
Their tongues extend to the Brahma heaven,
Their bodies emit countless rays of light;
For those who seek the Way of the Buddha
They show this rare phenomenon.
The sound when the Buddhas cough
And that of the snap of their fingers
Are heard throughout the whole universe
And the earth in six ways shakes.[6]

Buddha, as the unique one, is the center to which the devoted turn and to whom the worshiper bows. It is the Buddha on the altar, the figure. It is the one we can approach, sit by, and draw strength from.

It is also the Buddha of whom Rinzai says, "If you meet the Buddha, kill the Buddha"; the Buddha of whom Yasutani-roshi says, "Were the honored Shakyamuni and the Great Bodhidharma to appear, I would cut them down instantly demanding, 'Why do you totter forth? You are no longer needed!'"[7]

Transcendent, universal, personal, the unique one. Four Buddhas, but one world: which is the true Buddha?

Shakyamuni and Maitreya (the future Buddha) are but his servants. Now tell me, who is he?[8]

The word *Bodhisattva* is met almost as frequently as the word *Buddha* in Mahayanist or Northern Buddhist teaching, and the word *Bodhi* has close affinities with the word *Buddha*. Buddha, whose root is "budh," means to awaken, to recover consciousness, to recover from a swoon. Originally *buddha* was simply a title given to one who had worked on himself and had come to awakening. *Bodhi,* as we shall see later, means "to know," or better still "knowing," and a Bodhisattva is one on the path to awakening who has not yet come to full Buddhahood.

In Zen there are three important Bodhisattvas: Manjusri, whom we have just met, Avalokitesvara, and Samantabhadra. These three are respectively the Bodhisattvas of wisdom, compassion, and commitment.

Bodhisattva can also be understood in the four different ways. For example, Manjusri, the Bodhisattva of Wisdom, lived at the time of Buddha and was one of his personal disciples. The universal Manjusri is our own inherent wisdom. It is by the power of Manjusri that a universe is a universe, a teacup a teacup, a finger a finger. It is the intuitive perception of oneness as oneness and nondifferentiation. It is in this aspect that he comes to us in this koan.

In his transcendent aspect Manjusri is the teacher of Buddhas, as Mumon tells us in his commentary on this koan. Finally, in his unique aspect, he appears on altars in Buddhist temples, sometimes alone, sometimes flanking a Buddha image with the Bodhisattva Samantabhadra on the other side. On the altar Manjusri wields a sword, the prajna sword of wisdom which, it is said, cuts not in two but in one. Often he is depicted astride a lion, a symbol of the strength residing in prajna or wisdom.

Let us return now to the word *Bodhisattva* itself. As was said above, bodhi means "knowing"; *sattva,* on the other hand, means "being." We talk about *a* Bodhisattva, but in truth there is no such thing as *a* Bodhisattva. It is not *a* being that knows, but knowing/being. Our being is knowing: our true nature, Buddha nature, is knowing. "The one word *knowing* is the gateway to all mysteries," as one Zen master put it.

Knowing is therefore the basis of Mind. However, being is equally basic. Being does not arise out of knowing, any more than knowing arises out of being. We must therefore speak of knowing/being, a oneness which is a twoness, a twoness which is a oneness. It is like the inside and outside of a cup: we can talk of these as two, but both are one cup. We can talk of being and knowing as two, but both are One Mind. Philosophy, seizing hold of one or the other, comes up with materialism or idealism, saying on the one hand that mind and life are the outcome of matter, or on the other that matter and energy are the outcome of mind. Buddhism is neither idealist nor materialist, although it has been accused of being both. For example, someone asked Joshu, "What is Buddha?" Joshu replied, "The oak tree in the garden." Someone asked Ummon, another Zen master, the same question. Ummon replied, "Mind is Buddha." On the face of it, Joshu would seem to be reducing Buddha to the material world, Ummon to an idealist world. But this is but a superficial view. In a sutra it is said, "Form is only emptiness, emptiness only form."

But we must be careful as the ground is treacherous around here, filled with bogs and pitfalls, and one careless move will cause us to slip from the purity of knowing into the bog of knowledge. Knowledge is *crystallized* knowing, much like a pot is crystallized clay. For example, scientific theories, no less than the apparatus by which they are verified, are crystallized knowing. A product produced by a company is an idea crystallized in a form that has a demand. Language, music, and art likewise are crystallized knowing. Indeed, it is tempting to view all organisms, everything in the universe, as crystallized knowing: knowing whose being has hardened into form.

> "Like water and ice
> Without water no ice,
> Outside us no Buddhas," sang Hakuin.[9]

Knowing/being is our original nature. This can be verified through samadhi. In the Hindu tradition, deep samadhi is sometimes referred to as *sat-chit-ananda*, which means being-knowing-joy. We cannot fall from knowing, even though knowing may, and often does, manifest in discordant and confused ways: pain and anxiety, no less than joy and pleasure, are variations of knowing. Death may be the end of knowledge: all structures contain within themselves the primordial ambiguity and thus the seed of their own destruction. But death is not the end of knowing. Some teachers, in order to break the grip of crystallization, talk of "unknowing" mind, or "not knowing" mind, but this is like driving out poison with poison, and a very little is enough. The truth and good news is that we do not have to *be* something to know, nor do we need to *know* something to be. We do not have to be a body, brain, soul, spirit, or entity to know; nor do we have to know some secret, the content of books or teachings, the past or the future, the meaning of dreams and symbols, to be. Knowing/being is the preciousness in the jewel of life: it is "I am" and "I am" is the whole universe: "Throughout heaven and earth, I alone am the Honored One." But once we put it into words it turns sour and useless. What is this "I am"? "The oak tree in the garden," said one teacher "Dung," said another.

Some people say, "But if knowing is our true nature, what happens when we go to sleep and do not dream?" Sleep is not the loss of knowing, but its unfocusing from a center. Likewise the ambiguity of dreams is not the result of the cunning of some censor, but evidence that this unfocusing takes place. Deep sleep is pure knowing without content or form, without a center.[10]

Samadhi is somewhat like sleep. Ramana Maharishi calls it "waking sleep," and it has no content and no memory. However, in sleep there is no content in awareness because the mind is not aroused; in samadhi there is no content because the mind is fully aroused. Samadhi, which is knowing/being, is like moonlight (knowing) in vast space (being). Samadhi is not seeing into the infinite; knowing has a limit which is being. In other words, seen truly, the world is personal, concrete; it is only because we have abstract concepts that the world becomes remote and impersonal. The Chinese did not have a concept for the infinite, and so in the koan Momyo is not said to be infinitely far from Buddha, but one billion two hundred million countries away. The whole world is one body/mind.

Knowing/being as "one and two" is also encountered in early Greek writings and Western philosophy. For example, Parmenides said that "perceiving and being belong together in the same and by virtue of the same."[11] Plotinus said, "Intelligence and being are one."[12] Even Kant, the great champion of reason, says, "All life is noumenal only, not subject at all to temporal changes— neither beginning with birth nor ending in death."[13] And Hegel said somewhere that the real is rational and the rational real. Western philosophy, and also Tibetan, is divided into two main, and sometimes antagonistic, schools: epistemology, the study of knowing; and metaphysics, the study of being.

Knowing/being manifests as wisdom, love, and will, and so there are Manjusri, Avalokitesvara, and Samantabhadra, the Bodhisattvas of wisdom, compassion, and commitment, respectively. In the koan we are concerned with Manjusri, the Bodhisattva of Wisdom. Wisdom in Sanskrit is prajna, and Manjusri is therefore the personification of the wisdom that is inherent in all beings. The word *wisdom* has unfortunately come to have the implication of content and duration; we tend to associate wisdom with someone well-stocked with wise phrases and sayings. But prajna has no such connotation.

The *pra* means aroused or heightened, and the *jna* means awareness.[14] The Diamond Sutra says one must "arouse the mind without resting it upon anything." To arouse the mind, prajna, means arousing it moment by moment, flash by flash. The image of Manjusri on a lion wielding a sword is the picture of this flash by flash; he is a lightning flash caught in the act for whom the blink of the eye is one whole day. Like a catalyst, he transforms a galaxy of diversity into one fist held high. With one sweep of his prajna sword houses are houses, cars are cars, and trees are trees.

Prajna is aroused awareness, but not of "something": something would imply content, something that the mind is resting upon. Prajna is pure awareness of awareness, awareness seeing into itself. There is *no entity,* however subtle, that is aware of being aware; nor is there any being, however attenuated, of which there is awareness. It could be said that prajna is seeing into emptiness, or much better still, that it is seeing as emptiness.

The most celebrated of all sutras in the Zen tradition is the Prajna Paramita Hridaya, which means "the heart of the teaching on prajna as the way beyond suffering." It begins:

> The Bodhisattva of compassion
> From the depth of prajna wisdom
> Saw the emptiness of all five skandhas
> And sundered the bonds of suffering.
> Know then:
> Form is only emptiness,
> Emptiness only form.[15]

The five skandhas are the senses, feeling, thought, volition, and consciousness. All are seen through as empty, as having no essence or quality of their own. The skandhas are modifications of awareness, know-ing/being, and should this primordial awareness be aroused as prajna, emptiness is seen into. This does not mean that things do not exist. If we are aware of a chair, for example, prajna does not abolish the chair; it abolishes the delusion that the chair is something separate and distinct from awareness; that is, being is separate and distinct from knowing.

In addition to prajna there is another word, *jnana*, that is important to discuss. The *jna* of course means awareness; the *na* means primordial; *jnana* therefore means primordial awareness. Bodhi, as knowing, could be looked upon as the light source; jnana as the light diffused. The senses, including the intellect as the sixth sense, are called *vijnana* in Sanskrit: *vi* means divided and vijnana therefore means *divided* awareness.[16] This division is brought about by manas, also known as the ego-making faculty. Manas[17] would have some correspondence to me-as-center/me-as-periphery, and is what D.T. Suzuki calls the double-headed monster that faces two ways.

Our language takes note of this divided awareness in our senses. The word *look* is passive, whereas the word *see* is active. We can look without seeing, but not see without looking. We can say, for example, "I was looking straight at it but did not see it." Then there is hearing and listening: at the movies, for example, one hears the background music, but rarely listens to it. One touches (passive) or feels (active); tastes (passive) or savors (active); smells (passive) or scents (active); reflects (passive) discriminates (active).

It is this divided awareness that the Buddhists consider ignorance and in the koan is referred to as the woman. It is important therefore that we understand divided awareness clearly. It manifests as awareness of everything in general, nothing in particular, *and* as awareness of nothing in general and one thing in particular.

Let us take an example: you are driving along the freeway: it is a nice day, the road is clear and dry; the radio is playing music you enjoy and there is not too much traffic. You settle down comfortably and the car moves along smoothly. You are aware of the road, the car, your body, the music, the countryside—in short, all that there is to be aware of comes into and goes freely out of the mind. But then a horn sounds, brakes squeal—in a moment your back straightens and eyes flash to the rearview mirror. Your awareness is heightened, you are alert and observant, attentive to what is going on. It is nothing—a car had pulled up too fast on the shoulder and a following driver had overreacted. Your eyes move away from the mirror, you settle down, your attention returns to the music, your back relaxes.

These are two entirely different ways that awareness manifests.[18] With the first you are a participant, an extension of the car, the road, the situation, identified with all that is happening. This identification is a kind of oneness, or contextual unity, a unity of interrelatedness. "I am" is dormant. It may be a very pleasant, hazy, lazy kind of state, or a grumbling, dreary kind of state. It has many emotional variations, and most people spend much of their time in this state of awareness.

In the second you are no longer a participant. What is happening is happening *over there*. The center is over there and you are outside it looking in, so to speak. The mind is roused and fixed. Let us call this *observing awareness,* and the other *participating awareness.*

As the drama of life is acted out, each of us is participant and observer, actor and audience. As long as we can alternate as now one, now the other, now observer, now participant, our life has an even flow. But when we try to be both simultaneously, with the complementary threat of being neither, crisis threatens and in the shadow of this threat we grasp for the center from which, as we have said, comes language and thinking. This center, it could be said, is Momyo, the Bodhisattva of names and words. It is by reason of the point without dimension that our thinking can become needle sharp and capable of ever more delicate surgical operations of the living ambiguity, giving ever more subtle variation to the basic theme of "I-it."

Furthermore, just as a film can give the illusion of movement through a succession of still frames, so the intellect is able to give the illusion of a living flow by an alternation of "I" and "it" framed in words and concepts. Thus the intolerable is made tolerable and participator and observer are able to come together like the unicorn and the lion in a reflective union. Out of this union the five skandhas are born. The birth, though, is a stillbirth, and even our salvation turns out to be a new damnation.

The center shackles us, but without it, if it should fall away, melt, lie to one side, we should be like Renée—free but damned, swimming in a sea of panic and guilt. With the center we are secure, but prisoners bound to a treadmill kept turning by our efforts to fix the center eternally and unmovably, an effort which we have said is doomed to failure because of the fundamental ambiguity.

How are we to set the restless mind at peace, how stop the wheel of life and death from spinning? How are we to rid ourselves of a life of eternal compromise, half-truth, conflict, and hypocrisy? How are we to banish the many faces of the basic ambiguity?

Some of us struggle with the body, some with the mind.

The body is a strange thing: it is me and it isn't me. It is a living ambiguity. Am I in and part of the body? Or is the body in and part of me? Or are we quite separate, rushing along on parallel tracks? Or are we wrong to talk about me the body?

I control the body down to its most delicate gesture, but have not the faintest idea how this is done. We talk about a woman "having" a baby, but perhaps the baby "has" the woman. When people look at "my" body, they think they look at me; but do they? One understands what the get-with-it group means when they say, "I'm getting into my body," and "I'm making friends with my body"—but, at the same time, it is a very funny thing to say.

Some people feel that, if they could only bring the body under control, they would be able at last to resolve this ambiguity that both frustrates and confuses and so find the rest they seek. So they start "training" the body: yoga, karate, t'ai chi, jogging, sports, dancing. The logic is the same: "Let us get 'it' under control, make 'it' do what it doesn't want to do, and it will be an *it* at last, subject to 'I,' the center."

There is nothing wrong with yoga, karate, t'ai chi, etc. What is wrong is the underlying motive. The true practitioner of these arts uses them as a way of expressing the ambiguity. The tyro uses them to break it open, to have "I" the controller and "it" the controlled.

Another, more subtle assault on the body is made in the name of the conquest of "craving." Because we are Oneness, our craving is always for Oneness: this craving is the fundamental hunger and thirst. Everything we do is an expression of this craving, which finds relief but not rest in uniqueness. All that we do can be seen as symptomatic of this *disease* of craving Oneness.

As an example, let us consider eating and fasting. Eating is a way of "becoming one with." This truth with its religious overtones has been known for thousands of years and is the basis of one of the most beautiful and profound of all religious ceremonies—the Mass. Our craving for Oneness can then develop into a craving for food and some people will try to eat their way to heaven. However, this eating simply affirms the body without resolving the basic ambiguity. Others, also from a craving for Oneness, will deny the body and undertake ascetic practices which almost always include fasting. The aim of fasting is to deny the body and so bring it under control as an object and thereby resolve the basic ambiguity. Yet others will oscillate between the two extremes, now fasting, now gorging.[19]

A similar reasoning underlies other forms of gluttony: for wealth, amorous conquests, profligacy, with their opposites of celibacy, poverty, and discipline. The dynamism is the same craving for Oneness conceived as possible by swallowing and consuming, or alternatively by denying the body so that it becomes an instrument.

Of course, this is not an attack on true spiritual fasting, which has many dimensions, nor upon leading a simple or celibate life. Spiritual fasting is part of a wider context; it is not always a desperate attempt to resolve frustrations that arise from the craving for Oneness. We crave "it." But "it" never was, because, as a Zen master said, "From the beginning not a thing is." We can neither achieve it nor give it up.

Someone asked a Zen master, "What is a drop of water from the source of life?" The reply was, "A drop of water from the source of life." But this drop is not an "it." Yasutani-roshi said once, "All that is real is my talking, your listening." It is not the things we crave that are the problem; it is not that we eat too much nor that we do not eat enough. Our problem is *that we crave.* The problem cannot be solved by "giving up" food. When I am hungry I eat, when I am tired I sleep. The way is not in eating rice rather than potatoes, wearing a robe rather than trousers, having a bald head rather than curls,

sleeping on the right side, the left side, sitting up, or
lying down. The way is not even in "giving up" craving.
"What is the way?" asked Joshu. "If you go towards it,
you push it away," said Nansen. Giving up craving is
pushing away Oneness. The way is our everyday mind.
The woman and Momyo—Momyo awakens the divided
mind from its sleep of identification, a sleep in which
Manjusri is only a dream.

How are we to set the restless mind at peace, how
stop the wheel of life and death from spinning? Some
struggle with the body, some with the mind. Increasingly popular in the West as a way of dealing with the
frustrations of ambiguity is meditation. There are many
pitfalls along the path of meditation, but there are two
principal ones: the first in which the meditator seeks to
be pure observer by suppressing the participator, the
other in which the meditator seeks to be pure
participant. In both there is the search for the One at the
expense of two; both dream of Manjusri, while true
wisdom remains impotent.

Different schools of thought have different degrees of
subtlety, but most are of the opinion that "ego" is the
problem and that if we could rid ourselves of "ego" our
life would be much smoother and more spiritual. Some
see that ego is a center of conflicting forces and seek to
integrate these forces in what might be said to be some
total integration. This approach is more psychological
than spiritual and we have already touched on some
aspects of this in earlier chapters. Others would get rid
of the center. One spiritual teacher, seeing that the
center comes from the opposition of participant and
observer, seeks a solution to the problem by letting the
center drop away through letting go of the participant:

> Teacher: You have to learn to look, not make an effort
> to look. Look at those hills. Marvelous, isn't it?

Student: Beautiful!
Teacher: Now, Sir, do you look at it with division?
Student: No.
Teacher: Why not?
Student: There wasn't a "me" to do anything with it
Teacher: That is all.[20]

"There wasn't the 'me' to do anything with 'it'" means that there was no participant and so there was no conflict. This is the basic thrust of this teacher. He says, "I can only see what is when the one who sees (the one who participates) is not. This one only comes into being when you want to change what is." In other words, when you enter the situation as a participant as well as an observer; when you are two and not one.

This teacher says, "That center is the 'me and the not-me,' that center is the observer, the thinker, the experiencer [which he seems to regard as synonymous], and that center is the observed."[21] This is very true. But then he says, "Can the center be still or fade away? Can that center be absorbed?"[22] When Renée's center did this, she went mad and spent hours and hours and hours staring at a spot, at a drop of water, a speck of dust, desperately trying to get it back. It is not suggested that this meditation will send one mad. The answer is simply: "No, the center cannot fade away, any more than one can cure measles by erasing the spots." We can try, and some people do, to live a life of observing and not participating, a life in which they become more and more rigid, uptight, and controlled by outside circumstances.

The reaction of withdrawing from tension, anxiety, and conflict by just observing and not participating is a natural one. At the movies, for example, if tension reaches a certain pitch the audience will withdraw and say, "After all, it is only a movie." People who have been involved in a serious accident often report that they could see it all happening as if from outside: or "I was beside myself with fear." What is unnatural, however, is to turn this into a way of life. People walk around zombie-like, "maintaining awareness" as they put it, holding themselves aloof from hassle and conflict. They walk with eyes down so that they will not be distracted from maintaining awareness, and have no sense of humor, humor being grounded in the ambiguous. They often have an obsession with order and with obeying rules.

The other and opposite solution adopted by meditators is to let go of observing and sink into the center, into the "here and now" to become just participator.

The meditator sits quietly and expands his ego-consciousness to a larger scale. He feels one with others and shares that feeling and happiness with others. That is the technique. During the meditation period he holds nothing in his mind. When there is no ego-consciousness in the mind, at that moment he is able to become one with others, aware of others. Now he sits quietly, forgetting everything, the past, the present, and the future. He forgets the ego, expanding his consciousness to include everybody. He expands his ego-consciousness larger and larger and larger, joining all things together until all life is able to become one. He and others are not different, but are one in the egoless consciousness. In the end there is no boundary, no expansion, because he and others are one. From this awareness of oneness, he develops feelings of universal love and compassion.[23]

This is not good advice and Zen masters warn against this kind of meditation time and time again, calling it "the deep pit of tranquility," "the cave of demons," and "dead-void sitting." It makes the meditator torpid and dull, disinterested in life and full of inertia. He wants to sit all the time in quiet and darkness.

In contrast, Zen master Po-shan says:

> When working at Zen, the worst thing is to become attached to quietness, because this will unknowingly cause you to be engrossed in dead stillness. Then you will develop an inordinate fondness for quietness and at the same time an aversion for activity of any kind. Once those who have lived amidst the noise and restlessness of worldly affairs experience the joy of quietness, they become captivated by its honey sweet taste, craving it like an exhausted traveller who seeks a peaceful den in which to slumber. How can people with such an attitude retain their awareness?[24]

Sinking into being pure participant is also a natural reaction to intense stress. During moments of profound grief, for example, one sinks down and just "is" for a while. Inmates of concentration camps had the experience of "lying on the bottom." During intense and prolonged bombing, one lets go and drifts with the confusion and sound in a kind of pseudo-samadhi.

Both extremes, observing and participating, simply "get rid of" ego by a trick. Both, if used as a form of meditation, lead students to resent the "interference" of life with their "practice": on the one hand, seeing life more and more as a meaningless parade, scorning people who participate and get involved; and on the other hand, feeling more and more put upon by things, feeling increasing self-pity and seeking quiet—or paradoxically, seeking intense orgiastic situations such as acid rock, strobe lights, drugs, or the rallies of demagogues and faith healers.

One bird on the peepal tree,

One eats the fruit
The other looks on.[25]

The way is as treacherous as a quagmire, and although one can read books and get some beginning instruction, nevertheless after a short while contact with a teacher becomes imperative and the teacher must be good.

But who is a good teacher? Manjusri, the teacher of all the Buddhas, or Momyo? Manjusri is the teacher of the seven legendary Buddhas. How can the lesser teach the greater? How can a Bodhisattva who is not yet a Buddha teach a Buddha? How could Momyo awaken the woman when Manjusri could not? A commentator gave what he called a "Sunday-school explanation": "A child is crying: Christ, Buddha, Socrates, or Confucius all do their best, but the child continues to cry. Along comes an old toothless granny and with a few words the child is quiet and happy again." Well, . . . perhaps. But there is something much more profound at stake. If you want to get to Oneness, do you go by Oneness or twoness? By intuition or by discrimination?

Mumon says, "The drama old Shakya (Buddha) puts on is just a farce. Tell me now, Manjusri is the teacher of the seven Buddhas—why could he not get the woman out of samadhi when Momyo, a beginner, could? If you can firmly grasp this point, then for you this busy life of ignorance and discrimination will be the life of the Dragon Samadhi."[26]

It is said that the woman's name in Japanese is Rii, which means "separated from will or consciousness"—we would say, separated from the center.

Mumyo means "unawakened" in Japanese, but in the original sutra the Sanskrit name meant "throwing off all shadowy coverings." How can "unawakened" mean "throwing off all shadowy coverings"? Is Momyo the awakened one or unawakened one? Sometimes he is called the Bodhisattva of discrimination, the Bodhisattva of names and words. Manjusri is Oneness, or prajna—that is, no discrimination. He says, "How can a mere woman be next to Buddha and I cannot?" He cannot awaken her. Momyo walks right up and with one flick of the finger she is awake. Do you go to Oneness by Oneness or twoness? By prajna or discrimination? High is not high and low is not low—or is it?

Buddha, Manjusri, the woman, Momyo. How are we to understand them? As a hierarchy with Buddha at the top, then Manjusri, then Momyo, then the woman? Is Buddha superior to Manjusri? Is Manjusri superior to Momyo? Is the woman close to Buddha? How can Momyo awaken the woman and Manjusri not?

It's a dance, a square dance: "Take your partners all in a row, Buddha and Manjusri, woman and Momyo: round and round and then to the center, off we go. Change your partners, Buddha and the woman, Manjusri and Momyo."

But not Momyo and Buddha? Not Manjusri and the woman? Is Momyo too far from Buddha? Can anyone be too far from Buddha? Someone said that if the fool persists with his folly, he becomes wise. If the wise man persists in his wisdom, he becomes a fool. Is Manjusri too close to the woman, is that why he could not awaken her? The woman is in samadhi: how can she be awakened from samadhi? Is there anything alive that is not in samadhi? Mumon says that "if you can see into this koan your busy life of worldly affairs is a life of deepest samadhi." How can a woman, separate from consciousness and will, be in samadhi, how awakened from samadhi? How can Momyo awaken her, why can Manjusri not? Hui-neng says, "With a single ignorant thought, prajna instantly comes to an end. With a single wise thought, prajna instantly arises." In Buddhism, awakening is all, and Buddha is the Awakened One. But awakened from what? Awakened to what? In the Diamond Sutra is stated:

> Thus shall you think of this fleeting world:
> A star at dawn, a bubble in a stream,
> A flash of lightning in a summer cloud,
> A flickering lamp, a phantom and a dream.[27]

Is this what it is all about? We awaken from the dream? Or do we awaken *to* the dream? Did the woman awaken from a dream or to a dream? Did the woman waken from Manjusri's dream to Momyo's? What is Momyo's dream? What is Manjusri's? Is Buddha too a dream?

Someone said to Nansen, "All is One! Isn't that wonderful?" Nansen pointed to a flower and said, "People see this flower as if in a dream."

Yasutani-roshi said, "All that is real is me talking, you listening." How many are there? Yasutani and me, Yasutani or me, neither Yasutani nor me? Is it a dream, or not a dream? Are there things, no things, form, emptiness, Buddhas, Buddhalands?

> Let me and the world be as they are.
> There are no things, nor is there emptiness.
> If there are things, they are not for me.
> If there is nothing, I don't want it.
> I am no Manjusri or great brain.
> I am an ordinary man who does what he has to do.
> How simple is truth!
> *In the senses, thoughts and feelings lies true wisdom.*
> *Everything is one with Oneness.* [emphasis added]
> That which "comes to" is not two.
> If you want to be free from suffering and live in knowing
> I cannot tell you where the land of Buddha is. [28]
>
> —Layman P'ang

10

Arouse the Mind without Resting It upon Anything

A monk once asked master Joshu, "Has a dog the Buddha Nature or not?" Joshu said, "Mu!"[1]

Joshu said, "Mu!" Literally Mu means "no."

On top of a hundred-foot pole an iron cow gives birth to a calf. At the top of the pole of uniqueness, at the very center of centers, pinned there by language, the Gordian knot, endless in its entanglement, is even so sliced through in a single stroke: not to cut it into two, but to bring it to life. The iron cow of ambiguity yields new life in a single syllable. Mu! Is it one, is it two? The cave of demons is crushed. Does a dog have the Buddha nature or not? Mu! All our thought and theory can get us to the top, but how to take that fateful step to death which is resurrection? A camel can get through the eye of a needle sooner than a man rich in opinions, beliefs, credos, and learning can get from the top of a hundred-foot pole.

Let us not say that pondering and reflection, clarifying and reason are a waste of time. On the contrary, with their aid we can finally cut off all escape routes. We can finally see it is unequivocally one, unequivocally two; that the only solution is to establish a unique center, but that this center is then the stake to which, like a blind donkey, we are tethered and pass our life in an endless trudge of useless suffering. Reflection will show us the miraculous power that language has to liberate us to unending tyranny; and it will show us enough to allow us to doubt even that we doubt. It is said that when Buddha came to awakening, he sat under the Bo tree of prajna wisdom, and after awakening sat under the tree of worldly knowledge. In working on ourselves we cannot go far without Manjusri, nor can we go far without Momyo.

We never finish our work on Mu. There is no beginning to practice, nor end to awakening. There is no beginning to awakening nor end to practice. Each koan is a new slant on Mu; if we see into Mu we see into all koans. In practice, Mu comes first. When we see into Mu we see into all things, because all things are Mu. Mu is the magic center because Mu is Oneness; Mu is Sei and her soul and Gutei's finger. But what is Mu?

A monk asked Joshu, "Has a dog the Buddha nature or not?" Joshu said, "Mu!" On another occasion Joshu answered, "Yes!" Which is the true answer?

This encounter of Joshu and the monk is reminiscent of Buddha's encounter with the Hindu tradition. Embodied in this tradition is the notion of an individual "atman" or soul. Buddha taught *an*atman, no individual soul.

To get some appreciation of how radical Joshu's response is, one could imagine someone asking, say, St.

Francis, "Has the lowliest of tramps a soul?" And St. Francis saying, "No."

All beings are endowed with the Buddha nature. There is none who cannot become Buddha.

> Wonder of wonders!
> Intrinsically all living beings are Buddhas, endowed with wisdom and virtue.[2]

This was Shakyamuni's exclamation when he broke through to awakening. This is fundamental to Buddhism and is basically the only article of faith necessary for practice. What is the meaning then of Joshu's "Mu!"?

We do not know what was in the monk's mind when he asked this question. Was it that he was pedantic and had some doctrinal concern that he wanted to satisfy? It is unlikely, because Joshu had a way of handling verbal questions, questions without substance. Was the monk then looking for some inspiration from Joshu? It would not matter what the question was as long as he got Joshu to respond. Or was he perhaps lonely, anxious, somewhat lost, doubting his ability to come to grips with what he was not sure he had to come to grips with, and groping for some way, however inadequate, to express his bewilderment?

Does a dog have the Buddha nature or not? A dog was, in Joshu's day, the lowest of the low in the animal world. Something like a pig or rat in our day. Does even a rat have the Buddha nature?

It is said I am this wondrous and mysterious source. But how can this possibly be? My life is so disordered and full of darkness; it is an uncertainty made tolerable by looking forward to things of no real consequence and hoping while knowing that even the fullest satisfaction of my wildest hopes would mean no respite at all. How can it be said that I am endowed with all that can be wished for, that I am at the very source of the fountain of eternal youth and life? Each day is a struggle against being submerged in a restless stream of humanity that flows from the impenetrable chasm of the womb to the inscrutable abyss of the grave. Do even I then have this Buddha nature? If a dog has it, do I have it? It is bewildering. It is said there is this self-luminous intelligence, a vital creativity, and even a dog, a pig, a rat, even a scuttling cockroach, has this Buddha nature.

Religions always proclaim Hope. "Christians awake! Salute the Happy Morn!" The happy morn when tidings of comfort and joy are spread around. Faith, Hope, and Charity, the supernal triad of human resurrection from the death of confusion to the everlasting life of.... "Does a dog have the Buddha nature?"

If a dog does not have it, where then is Unity? Is Gutei wrong after all? If one dog has slipped off the raft, then is it truly a Great Vehicle? If faith, then faith. Can faith have exceptions? If Oneness, then Oneness, there are no exceptions. But then why does he say no? Do I have the Buddha nature? Yes. Does Hitler have the Buddha nature? Mu! Is this then Calvin's shattered world of the elect and the damned? If so, then what must I do to be among the elect? The British sailors have a saying, "Pull the ladder up, Jack! I'm aboard the lifeboat." Is there a chosen race, a chosen few—me but not thee? Is heaven for the unique, and if so will it not be lonely, will not one be anxious and lost in heaven?

One lost sheep and we are all lost, because is there not One flock, One Shepherd? If a dog is expendable, then why not a cow; and if a cow, why not a horse, a stranger, a neighbor, my son? Why not me? If one is expendable, all are expendable. Does a dog have the Buddha nature? Gutei raised a finger. Wonder of wonders, even the lowest and meanest, even a scavenging mangy dog, limping with dainty paws, ears flat, and incurled tail clasped between trembling hind legs, has the Buddha nature.

The import of this is so great that we overlook what it means. All without exception: young or old, beautiful or ugly, ignorant or learned, black, yellow, red, or white, all beings: Gandhi, Schweitzer, Einstein, Hess, Himmler, Hitler, the condemned prisoner, all beings are endowed with the Buddha nature, all are potentially Buddha. Even the monk, somewhat bewildered, concerned, full of words and sayings from Buddhist texts, full of questions and doubts and yearning for some reassurance, even he is a manifestation of this radiant, unborn, undying, serene, vast, and compassionate intelligence.

Does a dog have the Buddha nature? Mu!

Why does he say that? Was Joshu not serious? But if Joshu is not serious, who is? He had spent a lifetime of hard work having come to early awakening and had spent years, forty years, with Nansen, and a further twenty years visiting other Zen masters and monks, perfecting his awakening. If he is not serious, then who is? If Joshu was not serious when faced by this monk—it does not matter whether the monk was young or old, "advanced" or a novice—then where could the monk go? Where can any of us go?

Joshu was not faced by a monk but by a question. Not even a question. He was faced by a mind locked in its own embrace. It does not matter about the words: Does a dog have the Buddha nature? Is there a God? Is there life after death? Is there a meaning to life? Is an enlightened man subject to karma? The words do not matter. Each of us stands before Joshu and when we do so, we drop off our superficial baggage of being a man or woman, Canadian or American, in Montreal or New York, in 1982 or 982, we are caught in the vortex of our own bewildered and bifurcated mind, mortally wounded by a spiritual wound. Joshu did not have before him a monk to whom he gave a reply. It was like a rocket homing to its target. What is it all about? Bang! Emptiness met Emptiness. Mu!

> What is it? The question asks too much.
> What is? Still too much.
> What? Why so many words?
> ?
> Mu!
> !

The cosmic dance of mystery and revelation absorbed in '?!' Light years absorbing light years of galactic travel among galaxies that exceed the number of atoms in one vast compassionate universe in which even a dog has the Buddha nature. A world of such brilliant significance that even the sun is a dim candle in comparison. A Zen master said, "If you have one speck of dust you have it all. See through one speck of dust and you see through it all." Joshu's Mu! is one with the greatest, one with the least. But what is this Mu!?

Question and answer, doubt and affirmation. Which is the true Buddha nature? Is an awakened man nearer to Buddha than an unawakened one? Each of us has our own question. Question and life are one. Life is a response to the question. Our question is our karma and the monk's karma came to a head when he asked his question. Another's comes to a head when he asks, "Is an enlightened man subject to the law of karma or not?" Another's when the brightness of mind is confronted with the blackness of Mind. It is our fundamental question that separates us from others, but it is a doorway through which we must pass to oneness with all. Once when Joshu replied yes to the question about the dog, a monk persisted and asked, "Why should something with Buddha nature enter a hairy thing like a

dog?" Joshu replied, "Because of karma." He could
equally well have said, "That's the dog's problem." A
monk once asked a Zen master, "Where is my treasure?"
The master replied, "Your question is your treasure."

Joshu's response is dynamite. It is an invitation to
break through the protective crust of words to awaken
sleeping doubt. "Is my nose on my face?" Mu! "Is the sky
above and the earth below?" Mu! "Are roses red and
violets blue?" Mu! What is this Mu! To say it is "Yes and
no" would be like putting Manjusri's lion in a circus cage.
To say that Mu is a paradoxical response to heighten the
obviousness of "yes" is like taking Manjusri's sword and
blunting it against the rocks.

Someone protested, "But Mu is a meaningless sound."
How can any sound be meaningless, how can even a
speck of dust be meaningless? If Mu is a meaningless
sound, where is meaning? Where in a universe so vast
that it is now seen to be 1,000,000 times more vast than
ever before imagined, where in all this immeasurability
could there be one meaningless sound? Buddha once
asked, "If the bell stops ringing, do you stop hearing?" If
the bell stops ringing, does the dog stop hearing? What
is it that hears the bell? What is it that does not hear the
bell? What is Mu!? If one thing has meaning, all things
have meaning. If one thing has no meaning, all meaning
is lost. What is Buddha? Wash the dishes. How can Mu
be meaningless?

But, someone says, what if this monk has done
everything and nothing has worked? What if he has
asked and knocked and bashed and rammed. What if one
by one his companions of the night have left him:
ambition, pride, lust, knowledge. What if they have all
gone. What if during some extended retreat he got
serious and banished the shadows to find just nothing.
Not emptiness, sunyata, void, but nothing. It is like
waiting in a doctor's waiting room: there are magazines,

people, murmuring voices containing some hidden menace: and there is nothing, hanging there like a balloon. Everything is dry. Dry bread. The deep question, painful though it was, had some juice. Fear and anxieties offered something that could be chewed on. The hope for awakening, even though more sterile than a gelding, did nevertheless beckon. But what if the monk had passed all that and long ago the road had petered out, along with the signposts and milestones, and now there is just dust, dry, sere, and burnt, where there is not even the sound of dry grass rustling? What if the chest is sore, the belly hard, the breath uninspired, while the head aches and the shoulders are bowed under a weariness of posture long since past offering anything but more weariness? What if life seems to have gone on vacation and the question Mu is buried under all the endless dust?

Then our journey has begun at last.

The price for Mu is everything and we cannot pay this price with our feet up in front of the fire. It must be paid in that place where there is nothing, and to get there we must pass through the desert.

It is only when we have climbed to the top of the hundred-foot pole, when we have found that what we thought was so fertile and rich is but an iron cow, that we can expect new life to be born. It is only in the desert that Mu can be found and each of us carries the desert with us. We are like a giant who has lain enchained behind stone walls ten feet thick, lulled in imprisonment by whiffs of freedom feeding dreams of escape. Suddenly the wind drops, the whiffs vanish, and the dream fades away. Here is the bare truth. Now, relenting in no way, we get to our feet, snapping the chains without a thought, put one foot forward, the other, up against the wall, into the wall, be it concrete, iron, or steel, ten, twenty, or a hundred feet thick; we walk on unflinching, looking neither to the right nor left, without hurry or strain; we walk through and on. What do you say to a monk whose practice is as dry as dust from some forgotten attic? "Walk on!"

A monk asked Ummon, "What is the Way?" Ummon said, "Go!"

Mu is not a recent experiment that someone is trying out. It is not a shot in the dark in the hope or expectation that something might come of it. It is not simply for beginners or advanced people, for iron ladies or men of steel. Millions have worked with Mu over more than a thousand years: Chinese, Koreans, Vietnamese, Japanese, Americans, French, English, men and women, artists, professors, businessmen, farmers, homemakers, emperors, soldiers, airmen, monks, nuns. All have swallowed the red-hot iron ball of Mu, have perished in the Great Death while rejoicing in the Awakened life. Some have flung themselves into the furnace of Mu; some have impaled themselves on the point of Mu; some have drilled through emptiness and despair with Mu; some have dropped into the chasm of Mu. But all have found Mu to be home, to be that which they had sought since time began, but that which is more close than one's own skin. Some have gnawed at Mu like a rat that sharpens its teeth while gnawing through the wood of the vat to the butter beyond. Some have sat like a cat outside a mouse hole, to all appearances asleep, relaxed, indifferent, but all the while like a steel trap sprung open and ready to shut at the mere appearance of a whisker. Some have wooed, embraced, loved, and adored Mu, like a lover yearning and yearning and yearning. Some have held on to Mu like a lion at the neck of its prey, like a bulldog with jaws bred to clamp, to hold, never to yield. Some have penetrated Mu like a thread penetrating the eye of a fine needle. One found Mu in the midst of pain in the legs made a burning fire of agony by an accident, and another found it in the despair of forgetfulness when everything was finally lost in a samadhi of no hope and no tomorrow. But all have worked steadily, consistently. All followed finally what their teacher had been saying patiently, insistently, repeatedly: There is just Mu! Only Mu! Become one with Mu!

What is Mu? Our reasoning and thought can bring us to the door but it cannot help us through. All of our concern about Oneness and twoness, about the ambiguity, about the center and ego, all bring us to this point. Mu is the way. What is Mu? Mu is the question. Mu is the answer. Mu is Sei and her soul. If we see Mu simply as an answer, we shall hold it like some magic wand, waiting for it to turn darkness into day. We shall concentrate upon it, guarding it like some precious gem, but for all that we shall at best get to the top of the hundred-foot pole.

If we see Mu as a question alone—"What is Mu?"—we shall not know what to do in the desert.

Mu is not one. Mu is not two.

Arouse the mind without resting it upon anything. How easy it is to arouse the mind: "Let us buy a new car," "Let us get a new job or house," "Let us take up Zen." There are more ways of arousing the mind than there are drops of rain in a thunderstorm, but always the mind is resting upon something: "getting lots of money," "the neighbor's daughter," "a Christmas feast," "the solution to a problem." One thing after another, like paving stones down the road to hell, the mind hops onto this, that, and the other thing. There is always a center around which our life force whirls and down which it is sucked. Words and phrases bind the mind in boxes of absolute rest, boxes which go bobbing along the stream of time, buffeted and uneasy, across the rocks and rapids of opinion and disagreement.

It is also easy not to rest the mind on anything, to let go of the center in a soporific dream, in a paradise made of color, music, and shadows, in a temple of mammon and film stars, or before a box with an unblinking eye, or when we lie back on a soft bed in the warmth of sleep. Every night we accomplish this release in deep sleep without dreams. But the mind is passive. It is not aroused.

How do we arouse the mind without resting it upon anything? How do we pull ourselves up by our own bootstraps? How to jump over our own knees? Do the impossible, think the unthinkable? How to take that step, fertilize that iron cow?

> The gateway to Zen is Mu. So we call it the gateless barrier of Zen. Those who pass through not only see Joshu clearly, but go hand in hand with all the masters of the past, see them face to face.[3]

What is the difference between Om and Mu? Do we not concentrate?

It is felt that when a teacher imparts a mantra to a disciple he imparts at the same time some special property, either in the nature of prana or mana, the energy of oneness, that he has invested in the mantra; or in the nature of the mantra itself, in which case it is believed to have some special property which harmonizes with the basic pulsation of the disciple's psyche and so brings it to one-pointedness.

Is Mu then a mantra? It is certainly the function of Mu to bring us to one-pointedness. There is no question that without Mu as a dynamic center, or better still, the dynamism *toward* the center, we have no energy with which to work. In so far as a mantra is an aid to concentration, Mu is a mantra.

But that is the least of it. To say that Mu is simply a

mantra is to make the mistake of Gutei's assistant and Hui-neng's head monk. Concentration, no matter how intense, fierce, or protracted, cannot get us off the hundred-foot pole. Kapleau-roshi repeats and repeats, "It is not enough simply to hold on to Mu. You must penetrate right through to the very bottom."

It is said, great doubt, great awakening; small doubt, small awakening; no doubt, no awakening. Doubt is vital. We must open ourselves to the imponderable, the cave of darkness where the lion and unicorn strive in perpetual conflict. We must penetrate through the maze of yes, no, maybe, and compromise, past the back alleys of guilt and anxiety, to confront the beast or Minotaur that devours our freshest thoughts and most innocent of delights. The Minotaur is none other than the iron cow of ambiguity, the ambiguity of the snarling "me" torn like Janus, facing two impossible ways, lost between the Scylla and Charybdis of me-as-center/me-as-periphery. Great doubt, great awakening. It is not that we have to generate great doubt, it is not that we have to sit and squeeze like some great Rodin thinker until the great doubt is forced onto the stage. We just have to be honest. We do not know anything really. How do you raise a hand? You hear a sound: how is it that you hear? All the neurologists, biologists, scientists of all times cannot answer that. What is a thought? Who am I? What is a speck of dust? What is Mu!? We do not know anything. And yet our very being is knowing. What is thought? Mu is thought. What is Mu? If you see into one thing, you see into all.

The great doubt is aroused in meditation in circling around the center, in pondering and wondering. People who are afraid of thinking are afraid of the great doubt, no less than those who use thoughts as barbed wire to keep out the enemy called life. Once we have sacrificed infallibility, the nursemaid to uniqueness (not only our own, but the infallibility of all others); once we have repopulated the earth with ordinary men and women and have had them take off the many masks that elevated some to unique heights while banishing the rest to abysmal inconsequence; once we have recognized that the most cherished of statements, the most elevating of thoughts, the most eternal of phrases are but shifting pieces in an unstable jigsaw puzzle of probability that slips and slides while new pieces are made and old are lost, then we can think without danger and meditate with profit. Words cease to be opaque and are but windows onto the great doubt beyond all words.

But even meditation and concentration are not enough. Contemplation is also necessary, total absorption. What can one say of this? To become one with Mu. While Mu is "out there" we concentrate upon it. While it is "in here" we meditate on it. But what can we say when we contemplate Mu, when we are one with it? If you say this or that you lose it, but you do not come to it simply by not saying this or that.

The stakes are very high: life and death. But the way is not exalted, there is no bliss.

> To arrive where you are, to get from where you are not
> You must go by a way wherein there is no ecstasy.[4]

The redemption of truth from certainty requires that we "tread alone the bitter herbs of the elixir of life." Searching for an easier route, a quicker way, will simply lead us to stray into the enchanted arms of the sorcerer who, like a vampire, will drain us of our best hopes and vital energy. The Way is everyday mind, our most precious heritage. To allow others to use, which means abuse, our mind by filling it with empty phrases is to throw away that heritage.

What you do not know is the only thing you know,
And what you own is what you do not own,
And where you are is where you are not.[5]

A monk asked Joshu. . . . Mu! What is this Mu!? Wake up! Wake up!

11
Suffering Suffering

*A monk asked Tozan, "When heat and cold come,
how can we avoid them?" Tozan said, "Why don't
you go where there is no heat or cold?" The monk
asked, "Where is the place where there is no heat or
cold?" Tozan said, "When cold, let the cold kill you;
when hot, let the heat kill you."[1]*

Where is the place where there is no pain and sorrow? A
modern poet in the same vein as Tozan:

> The only hope or else despair
> Lies in the choice of pyre or pyre
> To be redeemed from fire by fire.[2]

That suffering is fundamental to life is the first basic
truth in Buddhism. The first sermon that Buddha gave
after his supreme enlightenment was on suffering. Life,

he said, is founded on suffering, all is suffering. The cause of this suffering, he went on to say, is the craving to be born. One might say this craving to be born is the craving to be "some one," unique and special. The word Buddha used was not *suffering,* but *dukkha,* which is often translated as suffering or pain.

It could also be translated as duality. Duality in itself is not painful; it is because duality is always seen against the backdrop, so to speak, of unity that it becomes suffering. It is the yearning for unity and wholeness beyond the separateness of life that causes the pain, a yearning that hardens into craving for an impossible unity conceived of as identity.

In Christianity, too, suffering is recognized not only as basic but as an essential ingredient of life. The central symbol of Christianity is the man suffering on the cross; the cross, it might be said, of duality: one yet two. In this crucifixion there is not only suffering and dissonance, but also harmony and beauty when seen against the eternal resurrection of the One. If there were simply the One, there would be no suffering, but where would be the life? If there were two, there might be life, but where would be the meaning?

In our very drive to be One we deny the One. In this drive to be One is the striving to be what we might call "good." All people strive to be good—even the most hardened criminal. A very hardened criminal once said, "Among themselves prisoners are human."[3] We strive to be good, not because the One is good, but because it is good to be one. Out of this arises our heaviest burden, the suffering of being human, a suffering we call guilt. It is in the denial of the One by striving to be good that guilt arises. In our effort to be good, we crush the good.

Zen master Nansen asked a governor of a province in China who was his student and who was leaving the temple after a period of seclusion, "How will you govern the people on your return?" "With wisdom and compassion," was the governor's reply. "Then every last one will suffer," said the master.

> If thou knewest how to suffer
> Thou wouldst have the power not to suffer.[4]

These mysterious words of the *Hymn of Jesus* echo the koan. How must I then suffer the heat and cold, the pain and the sorrow? When in pain, groan; when sad, weep! How must I groan, and how weep? If you knew how to weep, then you would not weep. Is there not already enough suffering that I must learn to suffer? Is there not, indeed, far, far too much?

Some cry out against too much suffering, cry out against an unjust or blind God or against an uncaring fate that sweeps us all along on the jolting journey of pain called life. But is there after all too much suffering, or too much useless suffering? But could there ever be "useful" suffering? To the average Westerner the very idea is absurd, masochistic. If there is pain, do something to be rid of it: take painkillers, tranquilizers, pot, booze, make love, write to your senator, demonstrate, or turn on the television. Do anything but suffer intentionally. Pain is, after all, isn't it, the ultimate intrusion, a foreigner insinuated into the tranquil state which should be free of all discomfort; it is something to be avoided, indeed something which can and which ought to be avoided. But what does one do when television, sex, alcohol, pills are the cause of pain? What does one do when one realizes that all is pain?

The Buddha said all is suffering, but sometimes it is hard to believe that he meant *this* pain of *this* moment. It seems so contingent, so easily avoidable, if only. . . . This feeling of loneliness, of fear, of confusion or humiliation, sadness, frustration, this feeling of injustice—does it too have a place in the All? And yet has anyone lived without it?

A woman went to Buddha with her child who had been bitten by a snake, because the child was dead. It had been a foolish mishap, a mistake. The child had wanted to play. Do not all children love to play, and do they not all love shining, colorful, quick playmates? Is this silver and green friend not someone to reach out to with a gurgle and tiny pointing finger? Now dead and growing so cold, so stiff, when but a short while ago. . . . The curse of fate, the accident of life. How could Buddha help? "I will help you; first you must bring me a mustard seed. Go and find one and bring it to me. But it must come from a house that has not known suffering." She searched. She could not find such a house. She returned to Buddha to ask him where could she find such a house.

> "My sister, thou has found," the master said,
> "Searching for what none finds, that bitter balm
> I had to give thee. He thou lovest slept
> Dead on thy bosom yesterday; today
> Thou knowest the whole wide world weeps with thy woe."[5]

What had the woman found? That suffering is good for one? That is but salt to a gaping wound. That suffering is everywhere? Yes, of course. But was that all? If so it would amount to little comfort. Did she perhaps also find that if Buddha were to take away her suffering he would at the same time take away her humanity? "You can hold yourself back from the suffering of this world," wrote Franz Kafka. "This is something you are free to do, and is in accord with your nature; but perhaps precisely this holding back is the only suffering you might avoid."[6]

"If you knew how to suffer." Is there more than one way to suffer? The wheel of birth and death turns and churns out pain again and again. Could there be suffering to end suffering?

> Seeing what I suffer
> Thou sawest Me as suffering.[7]

It could be said that this wheel of birth and death has suffering as its spokes radiating from "I" as the hub, the unique center which is off center. The "I" never quite makes it and from this "never quite makes it" come six ways of facing this truth. The turning of the wheel in time makes for six ways of suffering. The wheel turns always, sometimes this spoke, sometimes that at the top; sometimes we suffer this way, sometimes that, sometimes choosing fire to save ourselves from fire.

Spoke One—Donkey Suffering

If you know donkeys, you know them to be stubborn, mute, patient, and heroic. It was on the donkey that Christ rode to his death and rebirth. Donkey suffering is that which makes for the ordinariness of life and its mundaneness. Donkey suffering is there in life like a crack at the base of a column that sways in the wind. A total insecurity:

> Willy was a salesman. And for a salesman, there is no rock to the life. He don't put a bolt to a nut, he don't tell you the law or give you medicine. He's a man way out there in the blue, riding on a smile and a shoe-shine. And when they start not smiling back—that's an earthquake. And then you get yourself a couple of spots on your hat, and you're finished.[8]

Sometimes it forces itself onto the center of the stage:

> I wake up in anxiety: like a fog it overlays all I do, and
> my days are muffled with anguish. Somewhere in the
> mind are crossed the wires of fear and lust and all day
> long nature's burglar alarm shrills out in confusion.[9]

An ebb and flow from the mundane to muffled terror and
back to the mundane; from a dryness without respite
along an endless stretch of road cracked and torn with
thistle and dry grass, to the scorching fury of anger.

A survivor from Auschwitz wrote that grief and pain
hide behind one another in our mind according to a kind
of law of perspective. Human beings can never,
ordinarily, be content not because of some incapacity for
absolute happiness, but because of an incomplete
comprehension of the complex nature of unhappiness.
This leads us to give suffering the name of its major
cause, whereas this suffering is a composite of causes
which are set out in an order of urgency. "And if the most
immediate cause of stress comes to an end, you are
grievously amazed to see that another one lies behind:
and in reality a whole series of others."[10]

With donkey suffering it is not just that there is pain,
but that it is *my* pain. *I* hurt. It is not simply that the very
nature of life, with its fundamental ambiguities and
dilemmas, is suffering, but rather *my* health, *my* job, *my*
enemies, which are the cause. "I hurt and it is your fault":
a simple formula for an atomic bomb.

Spoke Two—The Horror of the Situation

The woman, going to Buddha for help, was asleep in
her own suffering, the sleep of "I hurt." But going from
door to door seeking a mustard seed from a house that
had not known suffering, she wakens to a wider dream,
a dream of "there is suffering," a dream that for some can
become a nightmare of horror. We might be able to
muffle our own suffering by blaming others. But who are

we to blame if those we blame, or even hate, suffer as
we do?

> I am the enemy you killed, my friend.
> I knew you in this dark: for so you frowned
> Yesterday through me as you jabbed and killed.
> I parried: but my hands were loath and cold.
> Let us sleep now.[11]

Sometimes, in a moment of grief, anguish, or anxiety, I
emerge briefly from the immersion in suffering and see
pain all around. Then the world shakes like the set of a
second-rate movie:

> I see, I feel
> The vastness of the agony of earth
> The vainness of its joys, the mockery
> Of all its best, the anguish of its worst.[12]

Donkey suffering comes from the experience of oneself
as an island of suffering in an unfeeling, unyielding
world. But now this very world is awash in suffering, its
hard outlines lost in the ooze of universal hurt.

P.D. Ouspensky speaks of having seen in a town in
Russia, during World War I, two enormous trucks loaded
high with new, unpainted crutches. He said that in these
huge piles of crutches "for legs which were not yet torn
off there was a particularly cynical mockery of the things
with which people deceive themselves." Yet he is still
caught up in his own pain. The "cynical world" and the
"deceived people" are just the ones who will have to
support their pained and mutilated bodies on new,
unpainted crutches. When we glimpse this but for a
moment, then the cynical face becomes a brave mask
hiding a suffering face, and wars become wars to end
wars.

When this glimpse strikes home, one then yearns to do something, to find some strength no matter how inconsequential, to support a suffering world. It is only then that the dream becomes a nightmare and we really touch the bottom of despair because, try as we may, we can experience only our impotence.

Spoke Three—The Suffering on the Way

It is when we see that we cannot evade suffering that spoke three comes to ascendancy. Suffering is not just over there, it is not a mistake. A new car, a new job, a hairdo, a long weekend away from it all will not shore up the crumbling defenses that the acid of life has eroded. It could be that the form the suffering takes is an accident contingent upon the flow of events outside our control. Accidents do happen. It could be that some malevolent friend thrusts upon us his own pain in the form of a betrayal: people sometimes are cruel. It could be that some stray virus finds us a congenial host and feeds upon our liver or spleen: illness does come. But if the form is contingent, and there are many forms, the fact is not. When this truth stirs, when we see suffering as our own and others' heritage, when we experience our numbing impotence and find we are lost and the road gone, then a new suffering appears—the suffering of the Way.

> Midway this way of life we're bound upon
> I woke to find myself in a dark wood
> Where the right road was wholly lost and gone.
> Ay me! How hard to speak of it—that rude
> And rough and stubborn forest! the mere breath
> Of memory stirs the old fear in the blood:
>
> It is so bitter, it goes nigh to death;
> Yet there I gained such good. . . .[13]

"Midway upon this way of life. . . . " Midway, not in time or distance, but in experience. Some never reach this "midway"; others have scarcely left childhood when already they are midway on life's way, and lost. It is only when the way is wholly lost and gone, when we have been truly abandoned by hope, that we can say we have entered the Way. When darkness descends, the glimmering light of life only makes the darkness darker, and we can find no point of rest, no shelter from the storm.

> Go—not knowing where.
> Bring—not knowing what.
> The path is long, the way unknown.[14]

It is the struggle with this greatest of all paradoxes, this worst of all cosmic jokes, that is the entrance to the Way. Where there is life it is said there is hope, and yet we must abandon hope if we are to find Life. Christ called us to him and he promised us rest; but to get to him we have to take up the burden of our cross. The way has always been seen as steep, long, and weary. Death and rebirth are the way, and this death is a bitter struggle alone in the dark. Often we back off desperately and turn our back on the lesson of the mustard seed and wrench out from the black corner of our minds the death-dealing formula "I hurt, it's your fault." Again we thrash around and around, desperate gerbils on an endless treadmill of blame, shame, and regret, until spent and exhausted we sink again into the darkness of the rude, rough, and stubborn forest of the mind, called again by the voice of truth.

> My feet were muddy
> And burning where thorns had scratched them

But I had the hope of seeing you, none of it mattered.
And now my terror seems far away. . . .
When the sound of your flute reaches my ears
It compels me to leave my home, my friends,
It draws me into the dark toward you.[15]

The Way has a price which few of us recognize when
we set out, so enchanted are we by those first few notes
of the flute, that sweet taste of honey after the bitter bile.
We enter the Way in darkness, we pass through the
entrance and we are given gifts, consolations, "moments
in the rose garden," as T.S. Eliot would say. So great is
our relief that we can be bewitched and deluded in the
belief that these sips are the whole ocean. But to walk
the Way is to pay a price. The way is to

A condition of complete simplicity
Costing not less than everything.[16]

Each of us has the fatal wound; because of it each has
had to dodge, duck, and weave through life. It is not
because we are bad, but because we hurt so deeply that
we do so many foolish things. Each of us has built our
barriers, turrets, trenches, and dikes, staked out our
claims. But now we must pay, and the price is our
defenses. Each of us knows, and has always known, all
the truth, but through the distorted lens of "I hurt" it has
appeared as a bad dream. Each knows that he or she is
nothing, has never existed nor ever will exist, was never
born. But this truth, instead of being our birthright,
bestowing complete freedom, deathlessness, and pain-
lessness, is fractured back to us as our being a nullity, a
no-person, having less than insignificance, and we build
up sandbags of conceit, arrogance, self-confidence,
self-satisfaction. It is these bags of sand that are the
downpayment.

> When they get a glimpse of this concrete and perfect
> life of the spirit—which manifests itself in the com-
> plete absence of all sweetness, in aridity, distaste and
> in the many trials that are the true spiritual cross—they
> flee from it as from death. . . . They seek themselves in
> God, which is the very opposite of love; for to seek
> oneself in God is to seek the favors and refreshing de-
> lights of God, whereas to seek God in oneself is to in-
> cline oneself to choose, for Christ's sake, all that is
> most distasteful, and this is love of God.[17]

And what is most distasteful is to experience our own
nakedness.

What is inimical to the way is self-satisfaction, the
unwillingness to continue to pay the price. Sins, as one
teacher has put it, exist only for people who are on the
Way, and then a sin is what stops us, what puts us to
sleep.

> Sin is what puts a man to sleep when he has already
> decided to awaken. And what puts a man to sleep? Ev-
> erything that is unnecessary, everything that is not
> indispensable. The indispensable is always permit-
> ted. . . . Work consists in subjecting oneself voluntar-
> ily to temporary suffering in order to be free from
> eternal suffering.[18]

Self-satisfaction, no matter how far one is along the
path, dries up one's roots of vitality. There was a monk
who was satisfied with his spiritual progress and went to
an elder to boast of his attainments, which enabled him
to be at rest and free from temptation. The elder said,
"Go and pray to the Lord to command some struggle to
be stirred up in you for the soul is matured only in
battle." The monk after that prayed only that he would
be given the strength to continue the fight.

Spoke Four—Meeting a Teacher

Who is our teacher? There is an age-old adage which says, "When the student is ready, the master appears." There are many who, as it were, sit anxiously and await the arrival of the kindly old gentleman or lady who will wash away the tears and soothe the aches of life. But are we not always ready, all of us? Is not our teacher always at our elbow? When karma is ripe, the price is demanded: and the one who demands the price is our teacher, who is not always kindly.

Some people with time and patience may set up rooms for us to meditate in, or to dance in, or to pray in, according to the tradition. They might encourage a little, shine a little light, waft a little wisdom. Then in our craving for "something," our craving for the ultimate in help, we fall for such guides. There are many indeed who seek a love affair with a system or tradition and seek to espouse the teacher in a rigorously monogomous marriage. Sometimes the teacher falls for the illusion and dances to the tune of the students, playing the Divinity to their devotion. In this charade the other teacher standing at our elbow is overlooked, even pushed aside, because we see only a bad-tempered bank clerk or a testy typist. It is these who are our real teachers; they have their hands out demanding the price for our insensitivity, dogmatism, ambition. It is through this buffeting of the world and life, through its humiliation, that we learn the real lesson of life.

There was an elder of the church who, if anyone were to talk about him behind his back, would go to that person with presents, that is, if the person lived nearby. If the person lived too far away for a visit, the elder would send presents by a messenger.[19] There was another, a disciple of a Greek philosopher, who was commanded by his master to pay anyone who insulted him (the disciple). He had to do this for a period of three

years, and when the time was over the master told him
to go to Athens to learn wisdom. When the disciple
reached that city he met a man who sat outside the gates
insulting everyone who came and went. When insulted,
the disciple burst out laughing. The man asked why he
laughed and the disciple replied that for three years he
had to pay for this kind of thing and now it was being
given away for nothing. An abbot used to tell this story
saying, "This is the door of God by which our fathers,
rejoicing in many tribulations, enter into the city of
heaven."[20]

Life itself is our only teacher, life with all its
frustrations, confusions, contradictions, and humiliations—above all humiliations, that furnace of the soul
which melts and burns the dross of ego, revealing the
gold of Self.

> From the moment at which I succeed in no longer
> moving in my humiliated state, I discover with sur-
> prise that there is the "asylum of rest": the unique har-
> bor of safety, the only place in the world in which I
> can find perfect security.[21]

Gurdjieff on one occasion, when talking to some
American students, said that in America there is a saying
about "the pursuit of happiness" which showed that
people there do not understand life. Happiness, he said,
is nothing, simply the other side of unhappiness.
Suffering too is important because it is a necessary part
of life: without it one cannot grow. But, he said, when
ordinary people suffer, they only think of themselves
and feel sorry for themselves, not wanting to suffer. This
is self-pity. If one is a real person it is different. A real
person will also feel real suffering and will not try to stop
it in himself: it is proper. "Must suffer to know truth
about self: must suffer with will. When suffering comes

to man, must make intentional suffering, must feel with
all being, must wish with such suffering that it will help
make conscious, help to understand."[22] Work consists in
subjecting oneself voluntarily to temporary suffering to
be free from eternal suffering. It is in this way that all life
is a teacher and death the greatest teacher of all.

> Abbess Syncletica of holy memory said: There is labor
> and great struggle for the impious who are converted
> to God, but after that comes inexpressible joy. A man
> who wants to light a fire first is plagued by smoke,
> and the smoke drives him to tears, yet finally he gets
> the fire that he wants. So also it is written: Our God is
> a consuming fire. Hence we ought to light the divine
> fire in ourselves with labor and with tears.[23]

In the end our heart is softened a little, after we have
paid the price once, twice, ten times, even a hundred or
a thousand times. The fire has made us malleable and we
can truly give a widow's mite because we are resigned
in heart, resigned in peace, not in defeat.

> Resigned in heart
> To exposure to the weather
> The wind blows through me.[24]

Spoke Five—Encounter with Ourself

When we have broken out of "the enchantment of
past and future," encountered the horror of the
situation, shuffled out of the security of our barriers, and
paid a small measure of the enormous debt we owe, we
find that we are still not in the light. We are engulfed in
a new kind of darkness, the darkness of ourselves, and
we are smitten by a new kind of suffering—the suffering
of fear. The way is not the way of the crowd but of the

solitary one. Each step is a step away from the crowd and each insight is an insight into the crowd of that which we had called the self, our precious personality which is sustained by others, by our sustaining others, a precarious patchwork that is common property and not private glory. And when we encounter this vacuity, this nothing, we are filled with dread. Buddha himself encountered this fear:

> Why do I remain thus in constant fear and apprehension? Let me bend down to my will that panic, fear, and horror, just as I am, and just as it has come to be. So as I was walking to and fro that panic, fear, and horror came upon me. Then I neither stood still nor sat down, but just walking up and down I bent to my will that panic, fear, and horror.[25]

We begin to learn what the Way is about when we see the contradiction inherent in ourselves: not the contradiction of good and bad, right and wrong, but the contradiction inherent in even the least belief, the least thought. If someone asks, for instance, how I enjoyed a party that I attended the night before, I find I have to say it was fun and a bore, lively and dull, this and that. Try as I may, I cannot be honest because there are so many possibilities, but only one truth. I so often do not know what to say, but am called upon to speak. I hear people maligning me and know the truth of what they say, but know too this truth is so partial, so out of context; yet to explain this would itself be a lie. It is out of this that fear mounts. "Learning is never what one expected. Every step of learning is a new task, and the fear he is experiencing begins to mount mercilessly, unyielding."[26]

The Fear. . . locked together we toss through the

nights . . . this Fear is after all not my private Fear—this
is only part of it, and terribly so—but it is as much the
Fear of all faith since the beginning of time.[27]

"The fear of all faith"—who would have known that faith
could have so much fear? Who would have known that
fear is the substance of faith, that waking up in the
middle of this fear is awakening in the midst of
boundless faith?

What is it that ails, what is it that yawns ready to
devour? It is not a question of struggling but of
wondering what it is that one must struggle with or
against. It is precisely this question which in a moment
of clutching horror pushes us into a world without a
center, a world in which what gave us security is no
more. Heidegger speaks of this encounter with ourselves
as "dread." "Dread strikes us dumb. Because what-is-in-
totality slips away and thus forces Nothing to the fore, all
affirmation fails in the face of it."[28] In Japanese this is
called *makyo,* and fear is the face of makyo. It is a total
defeat of what we call ego, but at the same time a victory
for "I." "Fear not, 'tis I." But, and this is the terror of the
situation, it is not always obvious who this "I" is.

> If one is oneself one's god, then God himself, the will
> of God, the power that would destroy one's egocen-
> tric system, becomes a monster.[29]

This is the worst of all suffering, and we shudder away
before the monster has barely stirred. It is here that faith
must sustain us. Faith, not in something—because that
too is swallowed in the yawn—nor faith that we can
escape the worst, but faith that the worst is but the proof
of faith. The worst, the horror of engulfment, is but the
self encountering the self in darkness. Faith is that
darkness from which all light has its source.

Spoke Six— Suffering that Has No Name

Jesus wept.

There are moments when the poignancy of our condition, our all-too-human condition, comes home. For a short while our heart softens and we weep, but whether for joy or sorrow one is never sure. There is joy in the compassion and sorrow in the sheer inadequacy of all that we can do. Christ could raise the dead, heal the sick, and comfort the disconsolate, and yet he wept. Kannon has a thousand arms and a thousand eyes: arms to soothe and embrace, eyes to know the suffering; arms and eyes growing out of the need to assuage and comfort, growing out of the very suffering itself.

The Jataka tales are about Buddha's earlier incarnations. One of them tells the story of his going for a walk and finding a tiger's cub. It was at the edge of a very steep ravine, mewing and trembling. Deep down in the ravine was the tigress, gazing up, trapped in a place from which she could find no way out. In her desperation to join the cub she had exhausted her strength, and in a rage of frustration she stood, emaciated and weak, angry at her defeat. Buddha was moved to pity. Unless she got out of the ravine, the cub would die. For Buddha at that moment there was but one thing to do. He hurled himself into the ravine, offering himself as sustenance to the famished tigress.

The Bodhisattva of Compassion, with arms to embrace and eyes to know the suffering, suffers the pains of the world. "I am sick because the world is sick."[30] In sacrificing herself to the anguish of the world, she assuages her own anguish, which is the anguish of the world defeated, in an exhausted rage of frustration, trapped in the ravine of separation.

The painful climb up Golgotha, the dragging of a clumsy wooden cross, the humiliation and indignity, the sacrifice of the body to the hungry mob, and the transformation of this into a sacrament of mercy—in this the West has found a way by which the blind can see and the dumb are enabled to speak. For a few blessed moments the burden of the mystery which has no form, no articulation is laid to rest. It is perhaps in this way that Christ may be said to have taken on and so allayed the sins of the world: not by saying that which cannot be said, but by being that word which can only be spoken by life itself. Even on the cross the merciful One is born constantly: even at the very extremity, the Way is vast and open: iron itself is warm with fertility and life, and the fire of rage and fury is the delicate petals of a rose.

> And all shall be well and
> All manner of things shall be well
> When the tongues of flame are infolded
> Into the crowned knot of fire
> And the fire and the rose are one.[31]

Notes

Introduction

1. A well-known Zen koan.

2. Wayne Booth, *A Rhetoric of Irony* (Chicago: University of Chicago Press, 1974), p. 177.

3. Ibid., p. 36.

4. This "ultimate irony" has been expressed in the West as the "principle of identity" or more briefly A=A. It is striking that Heidegger, in his discussion of this principle, speaks of a leap in a way that is similar to the way Wayne Booth, whom we quoted earlier in the text, speaks of the leap that is a fundamental prerequisite to appreciating irony. Heidegger says, "In the course of our discussion this principle (A=A) in the sense of a declaration has become an advance in the sense of a forward leap. The leap starts in Being as the ground of existence and heads for the abyss. Nevertheless this abyss is neither an empty nothing nor is it dark confusion." (Martin Heidegger, *Essays in Metaphysics* [New York: Philosophical Library, Inc., 1960], p. 30.) This abyss, we shall attempt to show, is Oneness.

Chapter 1

1. Philip Kapleau, tr., *Mumonkan* (Rochester, NY: Rochester Zen Center, 1975).

2. Wing Tsit Chan, *A Source Book in Chinese Philosophy* (Princeton: Princeton University Press, 1963), p. 203.

3. R.H. Blythe, tr., *Mumonkan* (Tokyo: Hokuseido Press, 1966), p. 149.

4. Wing Tsit Chan, *A Source Book in Chinese Philosophy,* p. 260.

5. Ibid.

6. Ibid., p. 324.

7. William Shakespeare, *Macbeth,* Act V, Scene V.

8. N.K. Sanders, tr., *Epic of Gilgamesh* (New York: Penguin Books, Penguin Classics Series, 1960), p. 103.

9. Swami Prabhavananda, *Shankara's Great Jewel Ornament* (New York: New American Library, Mentor Books, 1947), p. 40.

10. Chang Chung-yuan, *Original Teachings of Ch'an Buddhism* (St. Paul, MN: Vintage Books, 1971), p. 65.

11. R.H. Blyth, tr., *Haiku* (Tokyo: Hokuseido Press, 1966).

12. Sanders, *Epic of Gilgamesh,* p. 103.

13. Philip Kapleau, *The Three Pillars of Zen* (New York: Harper and Row, 1966), p. 302.

14. This song is a popular song, beloved by cockneys singing in the pubs in the East End of London. It was almost an anthem for British and Commonwealth armed forces during World War II.

15. R.H. Blyth, *Zen and Zen Classics,* Vol. III (Tokyo: Hokuseido Press, 1970), pp. 53-54.

16. Philip Kapleau, tr., *Hekiganroku* (Rochester, NY: Rochester Zen Center), koan no. 11.

17. Quoted frequently by Philip Kapleau, source unknown.

18. Wu John, *Golden Age of Zen* (Taiwan: National War College), p. 176.

19. Philip B. Yampolsky, *The Zen Master Hakuin* (New York: Columbia University Press, 1971), p. 34.

20. Chang Chung-yuan, *Original Teachings of Ch'an Buddhism,* p. 19.

Chapter 2

1. Kapleau, *Mumonkan.*

2. Elmer O'Brien, *The Essential Plotinus* (New York: New American Library, Mentor Books, 1964), pp. 80-81.

3. Ibid., p. 85.

4. Ralph Griffith, tr., *The Hymns of the Rig Veda* (Boulder, CO: Shambhala Publishing Co., 1973), p. 470.

5. J. Mascaro, tr., *The Upanishads* (New York: Penguin Books, Penguin Classics Series, 1965), p. 10.

6. The Hwa Yen speaks of Oneness, of Li, and it is said,

"(Oneness) Li is a realm beyond sense perceptions, a realm grasped only by intellect or intuition. All principles and laws that dictate the events in the phenomenal world belong to this category (Oneness). Li is, therefore, the invisible controller of all events. Of all the different Lis, the Hwa Yen philosopher seems to have in mind primarily the Ultimate Li—namely, tathata, (suchness, thatness) either interpreted as the universal One Mind or as Emptiness." (*The Teachings of Hwa Yen,* p. 143). While one may well want to question the advisability of talking about "grasping" Oneness, the gist of this statement is used to show the relationship of what we are saying with the Hwa Yen teaching.

The following is taken from Garma C.C. Chang, *The Buddhist Teaching of Totality* (University Park: Pennsylvania State University Press, 1974), p. 149.

a) The nature of nonduality is beyond all: therefore it is neither outside nor inside.

b) While Li (Oneness) embraces all things with its total body, it by no means impedes the existence of this total body in one atom. Therefore to be outside is to be inside.

c) The dual nature of nonduality is omnipresent; therefore it is outside and it is also inside.

d) While the total body of Li exists in one atom, it does not impede the existence of this total body in other things. Therefore to be inside is to be outside.

7. Mascaro, *The Upanishads,* p. 101.

8. It has rightly been pointed out that raising the hand, not the fist, was the Fascist salute. However, within this context the distinction is not meaningful.

9. Bertrand Russell says the work of Marx "is a complete self-contained philosophy of the world and of human development; it is, in a word, a religion and an ethic." R.W. Clark, *Life of Bertrand Russell* (New York: Penguin Books), p. 77.

10. Jung wrote, "I can still recall how Freud said to me, 'My dear Jung, promise me never to abandon the sexual theory. That is the most essential thing of all!' . . . He said it to me with great emotion, in the tone of a father saying, 'And promise me this one thing: that you go to Church every Sunday.'" Ernest Becker, *The Denial of Death* (New York: Free Press, Div. of Macmillan Publ. Co., 1973), pp. 94–5. See also Eric Fromm, *Psycho-Analysis and Religion* (New Haven, CT: Yale University Press, 1950).

11. Dietrich Bonhoeffer, *Letters and Papers from Prison* (Huntington, NY: John M. Fontana Publ., 1964), p. 135.

12. Alfred North Whitehead, *Religion in the Making* (New York: Meridian Books, Inc., Living Age Books, 1960), p. 17.

13. Joachim Remak, *The Nazi Years* (Englewood Cliffs, NJ: Prentice Hall, 1969), p. 100.

14. Ibid., p. 96.

15. This search for the unifying Oneness is exemplified by the striving by Einstein and his successors for a unified field theory. The belief in Oneness is exemplified in the postulate of Einstein that "all phenomena of nature, all the laws of nature are the same for all systems that move uniformly relative to one another." This is a restatement in Western terms of "Li" (*see* note 6 above).

16. Roselle Chartok and Jack Spencer, *The Holcaust Years* (New York: Bantam Books, 1981), p.199.

17. J.P. Stern *The Fuhrer and the People* (Berkeley, CA: University of California Press, 1975), p.192.

18. Ibid., 192.

19. Ibid., 194.

20. Ibid., 163.

21. Joachim Fest, *Hitler* (St. Paul, MN: Vintage Books, 1975), p. 329

22. Ibid., 328.

23. Ibid.

24. This flash by which a confused and disordered area is reduced to order in an elegant and simple whole is well known in creative work. "During last night of 22–23 March 1892 around half past two in the morning the circular limit theorem as already prefigured by the fourteen-angled figure suddenly appeared before me. I now knew I had discovered an important theorem." Felix Klein, quoted by Marie-Louise Von Franz, Andrea Dykes, tr., *Number and Time*, (Evanston, IL: Northwestern University Press, 1944), p. 21. *See also* Brewster Ghiselin, *The Creative Process* (New York: New American Library, Mentor Books, 1952); Arthur Koestler, *The Act of Creation* (London: Pan Books, 1964); and Albert Low, *Zen and Creative Management* (New York: P.E.I. Books, Inc., Playboy Paperbacks, 1982).

25. Fest, *Hitler*, p. 328.

26. Whitehead, *Religion in the Making*, p. 17.

27. Rhue Morton, *The Wave* (New York: Dell Publ.Co.,

1981). This is a fictional account which, according to the publishers, is based upon fact.

28. Chang Chung-yuan, *Original Teachings of Ch'an Buddhism*, p. 68

29. James Robinson, ed., *The Nag Hammadi Library* (New York: Harper and Row Publ., Inc., 1977), p. 126.

30. Kapleau, *The Three Pillars of Zen*, p. 74.

31 John Wu, *The Golden Age of Zen*, p. 37.

Chapter 3

1. Kapleau, *Mumonkan.*

2. Elaine Pagels, *Gnostic Gospels* (New York: Random House, Inc., Vintage Books, 1981), p. 66.

3. R.W. Clark, *Einstein, The Life and Times* (New York: The Hearst Corp., Avon Books, 1971), p. 417.

4. *See* other examples of ambiguity in Albert Low, *Zen and Creative Management.*

5. Bikku Nananda, *Concept and Reality in Early Buddhist Thought* (Kandy, Sri Lanka: Buddhist Publications Society, 1971), p. 17. Also, p. 35: "In many a context it is said that the muni has abandoned all views. He has no views because he has got rid of the *point* of view, that is, the illusion of the ego."

6. Kapleau, *Mumonkan.*

Chapter 4

1. Kapleau, *Mumonkan.*

2. This figure is known to Freemasons and ancient architects and was called the Vesica Pisces. "So popular in the Middle Ages [it] was applied by the Masons in planning their temples. Albert Durer, Serlio and others depict the Vesica in their works, but presumably because of the unspeakable mystery attached to it these authors made no reference to it." "This mysterious figure Vesica Pisces possessed unbounded influence on the details of sacred architecture: *and it constituted the great enduring secret of our ancient brethren* (emphasis in original). The Vesica was also regarded as a baneful object under the name of the 'Evil Eye,' and the charm most generally employed to avert the dread effects of its fascination was the phallus. . . . To every Christian the Vesica is familiar from its constant use in early art, for not only was it the feminine aspect of the Savior as symbolized by the *wound* in his side, but it commonly surrounds the figure of Christ, as His Throne when

seated in Glory." William Stirling, *The Canon* (London: Garnstone Press, 1974), pp. 12–13. *See also* John Michell, *City of Revelation* (London: Garnstone Press, 1972), pp. 70–76.

John Michell also says the following, to explain some aspects of the Vesica: "In *Timaeus* 35 Plato began his account of the method by which God constituted the universal soul from the Same and the Other which, being naturally difficult to mix, were brought together through the medium of a third Essence." He then quotes the following from *Timaeus* and draws the diagrams: "And (He) bent either of them into a circle and joined them, each to itself, also to the Other, at a point opposite to where they had first been laid together. And he encompassed them about with the motion that revolves in the same spot continually, and he made the one circle outer and the other inner. And the outer motion He ordained to be Motion of the Same, and the inner motion the motion of the Other. And he made the motion of the same to be toward the right along the side, and the motion of the Other to be toward the left of the diagonal."

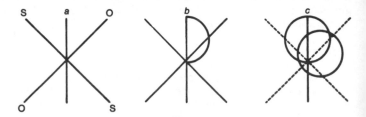

The Geometry of Creation

3. Rudolf Arnheim, *The Power of the Center* (Berkeley: University of California Press, 1982), p. 4.

4. Pierre Teilhard de Chardin, *The Phenomenon of Man* (London: Collins, Fount Paperbacks, 1959), p. 35.

5. R.D. Laing, *The Divided Self* (Gretna, LA: Pelican Publishing Co., Inc., 1965), p. 26.

6. This difficult point is mirrored in the Sufi tradition. Henry Corbin writes that the "transcendent dimension (which we call One) has a total structure, . . . that of a bi-unity, a *unus-ambo.*

This *unus-ambo* can be taken as an alternation of the first and second person (I-Thou) as forming a dialogic unity thanks to the identity of their essence and yet without confusion of persons. . . . One cannot understand this relationship except in the light of the fundamental Sufi saying, 'He who knows *himself* knows *his Lord.*' The identity of *himself* and *Lord* does not correspond to a relationship of 1=1, but of 1 x 1   It would therefore be as wrong to reduce the two dimensionality of this dialogic unity to a solipsism as to divide it into two essences, each of which could be itself without the other. . . . [the relation in this unus-ambo] each of the two simultaneously assumes the position of *I* and the *self* image and mirror: my image looks at me with my own look: I look at it with its own look." Henry Corbin, *The Man of Light in Iranian Sufism* (Boulder, CO: Shambhala Publishing, 1971), pp. 7-17.

7. Teilhard, *The Phenomenon of Man*, pp. 37, 39.

8. "The famous Gordian knot . . . is a long-standing symbol of the labrynth arising out of the chaotic and inextricable tangle of the cords with which it was tied. To undo the knot was equivalent to finding the 'Center' which forms such an important part of all mystic thought." J.E. Cirlot, *A Dictionary of Symbols* (New York: Philosophical Library, Inc., 1972), p. 164.

9. In the Pythagorean cosmogony is the "idea that the one, as monad, sometimes represents the one original arche of the world and sometimes reveals itself as the generating single seed (thus revealing only one side of its two anti-thetical series). R. Allendy calls 'the oneness of the one a synthetic element and the numerical one an analytic element.'" We shall be returning to this subject in the next chapter. Marie-Louise Von Franz, *Number and Time*, pp. 62-63.

10. Arnheim, *The Power of the Center*, p. 2.

11. Ibid, p. 12.

12. Anonymous, *Autobiography of a Schizophrenic Girl* (New York: New American Library, Signet, 1951), p. 40.

13. Levi-Strauss refers to dual or moiety organization of villages in some primitive tribes. When a researcher asked about village structure of the inhabitants of one village, most described the village as a circular village separated by an imaginary diameter running northwest and southeast. Several informants, however, denied that and said the village was arrayed concentrically around the lodges of the chief. These

two patterns of structure do actually exist and these structures could be called diametric and concentric. The first does not have a center, the second does; in the first there is a hierarchic relationship, in the second a relationship of equality. However, the question would then become: which moiety should occupy the center. In the description of the village, those who described it diametrically were the 'upper class' of the tribe: those who described it concentrically were the 'lower class.' To resolve the conflict some tribes consider their social structure in both diametric and concentric terms and by a simple mental operation: 'Each moiety can at will regard itself and the other moiety as either central or peripheral." Claude Levi-Strauss, *Structural Anthropology* (New York: Penguin Books, Classics Series, 1963), pp. 132–146.

Chapter 5

1. Kapleau, *Hekiganroku.*

2. Paul Buckley and F. David Peat, *A Question of Physics: Conversations in Physics and Biology* (Toronto: University of Toronto Press, 1979), p. 128.

3. Vidyakara, ed., and Daniel H. Ingalis, tr., *Sanskrit Poetry from Vidyakara's Treasury* (Cambridge, MA: Harvard University Press, 1968), p. 141.

4. Andrew Lloyd Webber and Tim Rice, *Rock Opera: Jesus Christ Superstar.*

5. Gerald Brenan and Lynda Nicholson, tr., *St. John of the Cross: His Life and Poetry* (Cambridge, England: Cambridge University Press, 1975), p. 49.

6. Ben Johnson, *To Celia.*

7. Edward C. Dimock, Jr. and Denise Levertov, tr., *In Praise of Krishna: Songs from the Bengali* (New York: Doubleday and Co., Inc., 1967), p. 41.

8. John Tettemer, *I was a Monk* (Wheaton, IL: Theosophical Publishing House, Quest Books, 1974), p. 117.

9. G.R.S. Mead, *Pistis Sophia* (London: John Watkins, 1963), p. 4.

10. *Bhagavad Gita,* Radhakrishna, tr., (London: George Allen and Unwin, 1948), p. 275.

11. Henry Corbin, *The Man of Light in Iranian Sufism,* p. 21.

12. Warner Allen, "The Timeless Moment," quoted in F.C.

Happold, *Mysticism* (New York: Penguin Books, Pelican, 1970), p. 133.

13. Author's own experience.

14. Author's own experience.

15. Chang Chen-chi, *The Practice of Zen* (London: Rider & Co., 1960), p. 122.

16. Ibid., p. 106.

17. Holmes Welch, *The Practice of Chinese Buddhism*, 1900–1950 (Cambridge, MA: Harvard University Press, 1967), p. 82.

18. Chang Chen-Chi, *The Practice of Zen,* p. 109.

19. Author's own experience. For more information *see:* Philip Kapleau, *Zen: Dawn in the West* (New York: Doubleday & Co., Inc., Anchor Press, 1979), p. 145.

20. Happold, *Mysticism,* p. 131.

21. According to Koestler, creativity arises out of "the perceiving of a situation or idea in *two self-consistent but habitually incompatible forms of reference*" (emphasis added). The resultant explosion may be experienced as humor, discovery, creation, or awakening. Arthur Koestler, *The Act of Creation* (London: Pan Books, 1964), p. 35.

22. Francesca Freemantle and Chogyam Trungpa, tr., *The Tibetan Book of the Dead: The Great Liberation Through Hearing in the Bardo* (Boulder, CO: Shambhala Publ., 1975), p. 37.

Chapter 6

1. Kapleau, *Mumonkan.*

2. R.B. Blakney, tr., *Tao Teh King* (New York: Mentor Books, 1955), p. 63.

3. These words are ambiguous, and as they are used frequently in the book, it will be as well to be aware of this ambiguity. *Unique* means both "the only one of its kind" and "of ultimate value." For example, to say that "the Bible is unique" might mean not only that one will not find its like anywhere, but also that it has a very special importance. The first is a statement of fact, the second of value. Meaning can also be understood in two ways. *Meaning* arises from a part finding its relationship within a greater whole, or it arises from something pointing beyond itself. Thus, for example, the meaning of a word is to be found within the context in which

it occurs. (The word *force* changes in meaning according to whether it is used in a scientific or political context.) The meaning of a symbol is derived from what the symbol points to. Finally, the word *center* can mean a geometric and geographical location, i.e., the center of a circle or the center of a town, or it can mean a dynamic center, which reconciles forces and tensions in a dynamic field. Generally speaking, the second meaning is to be assumed in each case.

4. Ernest Becker, who made uniqueness a fundamental theme of his book, *The Denial of Death,* says, "Man's tragic destiny: he must desperately justify himself as an object of primary value in the universe: he must stand out, be a hero, make the biggest contribution to world life, show he counts more than anything else." Ernest Becker, *The Denial of Death* (The Free Press, 1973), p. 4.

5. Mumon has a verse to the koan in the *Mumonkan:* "The mountain spirit raised his hand and lo, with little effort, the thousand myriad piled high mountain was split in two." Kapleau, *Mumonkan.*

6. Jung says, "Psychologically (the wheel) denotes concentration and preoccupation with a center conceived as a center of a circle and thus formulated as a point. . . . The center is the meaning shared by two extremes." C.G. Jung, *Aion* (Boulder, CO: Shambhala Publ., Inc., Routledge and Kegan Paul, 1959), p. 224. Becker says, "The development of the person is a development in depth from a fixed center in the personality, a center that united both aspects of the existential dualism." Ernest Becker, *The Denial of Death,* p. 80.

7. T.S. Eliot, *The Four Quartets* (Winchester, MA: Faber and Faber, Inc., 1944).

8. Rilke, "The Force of Gravity," quoted by Martin Heidegger, Albert Hofstadter, tr., in *Poetry, Language, Thought* (New York: Harper and Row Publ., Inc., Torchbooks, 1975), p. 104.

9. Elmer O'Brien, *Essential Plotinus,* p. 83.

10. "Man's character is a structure built up to avoid terror, perdition and annihilation that dwell next door to everyman." Ernest Becker, *The Denial of Death,* p. 70.

11. Communicated to the author by a Raja Yoga teacher.

12. Martin Lings, *A Sufi Saint of the 20th Century* (Berkeley, CA: University of California Press, 1973), p. 149.

13. C.G. Jung, *Aion,* pp. 220–221.

14. Quoted by Gyorgy Doczi in *The Power of Limits: Proportional Harmonies in Nature, Art, and Architecture* (Boulder, CO: Shambhala Publ., Co., 1981), p. 102.

15. George Leonard, *The Silent Pulse* (New York: Bantam Books, Inc., 1978), p. 104.

16. Quoted in David Hay, *Exploring Inner Space* (New York: Pelican Books, 1982), p. 90.

17. For more information *see* Albert Low, *Zen and Creative Management,* pp. 122–140.

18. Joseph Campbell, *The Hero with a Thousand Faces* (Princeton, NJ: Princeton University Press, Bollingen Series, 1960), p. 33.

19. Mircea Eliade, *Shamanism* (Princeton, NJ: Princeton University Press, Bollingen Series, 1972), p. 265.

20. Campbell, *The Hero with a Thousand Faces,* p. 42.

21. Norman Cohn, *The Pursuit of the Millennium* (Oxford, England: Oxford University Press, 1970), p. 64.

22. Most initiation ceremonies are accompanied by pain inflicted in one way or another. The effect of this pain is to "fix" a center. Pain is ultimate duality, and the center held in the midst of pain is "tempered," much as steel is tempered by being held in the fire. For example, when Buddhist monks in China made a vow of ordination, they might, at that time, burn off a finger.

23. Campbell, *The Hero with a Thousand Faces,* p. 44.

24. Anonymous, *Autobiography of a Schizophrenic Girl,* p. 30.

25. Gregory Bateson, *Steps to an Ecology of Mind* (New York: Ballantine Books, 1972), p. 208.

26. Anonymous, *Autobiography of a Schizophrenic Girl,* p. 21.

27. Ibid., p. 38.

28. Ibid., p. 75.

29. Ibid., p. 55.

30. Ibid., p. 84.

31. Ibid., p. 87.

32. Patrick Kealley, *Los Angeles Times,* reported in *Montreal Gazette,* March 1982.

33. Lama Anagarika Govinda, *Psycho-cosmic Symbolism of the Buddhist Stupa* (Berkeley: Dharma Publishing, 1976).

34. Kapleau, *Hekiganroku.*

35. Chang Chung-yuan, *Original Teaching of Ch'an Buddhism,* p. 296.

36. Tettemer, *I was a Monk,* p.117.

37. Kapleau, *Hekiganroku.*

38. Ibid.

39. Chang Chung-yuan, *Original Teachings of Ch'an Buddhism,* p. 23.

40. Ibid., p. 240.

41. Ibid., p. 242.

42. Ibid., p. 242.

Chapter 7

1. Kapleau, *Mumonkan.*

2. Ibid.

3. J. Krishnamurti, *The Awakening of Intelligence* (New York: Harper and Row, 1973), p. 129.

4. Isshu Miura and Ruth Fuller Sasaki, *Zen Dust* (San Diego: Harcourt, Brace & World, Inc., 1966), p. 54.

5. Helen Keller, quoted by Gyorgy Doczi, *The Power of Limits: Proportional Harmonies in Nature, Art, and Architecture,* p. 29.

6. Antonio de Nicolas, *Meditations through the Rig Veda* (York Beach: ME: Nicholas Hays Inc., 1976), p. 60.

7. Oswald Spengler, *Decline of the West* (Winchester, MA: Allen and Unwin, 1959), p. 123.

8. Tettemer, *I was a Monk,* p. 136.

9. Kapleau, *Mumonkan.*

10. I.A. Richards and C.K. Ogden, *The Meaning of Meaning* (San Diego: Harcourt, Brace Jovanovich Inc. Harvest Books, 1923), p. 35.

11. J.G. Frazer, *The Golden Bough* (New York: St. Martin's Press, Inc., 1957), p. 323.

12. John 1:1.

13. "The first and second person of the Trinity would be related to each other as the *thought* that leads to utterance is to the *uttered* word that expresses the thought. . . . What we say about words in the empirical realm bears a notable likeness to what is said about God in theology." Kenneth Burke, *Rhetoric in Religion* (Berkeley: University of California Press, 1970), p. 13.

14. *See* the work of Dr. William Condor: "Communication is

like a dance with everyone engaged in intricate and shared movement across many subtle dimensions." Quoted in *Omni Magazine*, December 1981, p. 18.

15. Lama Govinda, *Creative Meditation and Multi-Dimensional Consciousness*, p. 75.

16. Martin Heidegger, *Existence and Being* (Baltimore, MD: Geneological Publishing Co., Gateway Press, Inc., 1949), p. 278.

17. Ibid., p. 279.

18. Ibid.

19. Kapleau, *Hekiganroku*.

20. "The attitude of man is twofold in accordance with the twofold nature of the primary words which he speaks. The one primary word is the combination *I-Thou*. The other primary word is the combination *I-it*." Martin Buber, *I and Thou*, Ronald Gregor Smith, tr., (Edinburgh: T. & T. Clark, 1937), p. 3.

21. Lings, *A Sufi Saint of the 20th Century*, p. 127.

22. Ibid., p. 203.

23. Katsuki Sekida, tr., *Two Zen Classics*, (New York: John Weatherhill, Inc., 1977), p. 166.

24. René Guénon, *Symbolism of the Cross* (London: Luzac and Co., 1975), p. 18.

25. Lings, *A Sufi Saint of the 20th Century*, p. 150.

26. Ibid.

27. Esther Harding, *Psychic Energy* (Princeton, NJ: Princeton University Press, Bollingen Series, 1963), p. 199.

28. Adolf Hitler, quoted in Kapleau, *Dawn in the West*, p. 19.

29. Laing, *The Divided Self*, p. 20.

30. Burke, *The Rhetoric of Religion*, p. 19.

31. Anonymous, *Autobiography of a Schizophrenic Girl*, p. 33.

32. Ibid., p. 40.

33. Ibid.

34. Ibid. Also Martin Heidegger says, "When we are caught in the uncanniness of dread, we often try to break the empty silence by words spoken at random. . . ." Heidegger, *Existence and Being*, p. 336.

35. Ibid., p. 40.

36. Michael Harwood, "The Universe and Dr. Hawkins," *The New York Times Magazine*, January 23, 1983, p. 54.

37. Ibid.

38. Bertrand Russell, *Mysticism and Logic* (New York: Penguin Books, 1953), p. 70.

39. K. Ramanan, *Nagarjuna's Philosophy* (Boulder, CO; Shambhala Publishing Co., 1975), p. 161.

40. T. Stcherbatsky, *The Conception of Buddhist Nirvana* (New York, Samuel Weiser, Inc., 1978), p. 77.

41. R.H. Blyth, *Zen and Zen Classics,* Vol. II, p. 69.

42. Ruth Fuller, Yoshita Iriya, and Dana R. Fraser, trs., *The Recorded Sayings of Layman P'ang* (New York: Weatherhill, 1971), p. 47.

43. Chang Chung-yuan, *Original Teachings of Ch'an Buddhism,* p. 241.

Chapter 8

1. Kapleau, *Mumonkan.*

2. Flo Conway and Jim Siegelman, *Snapping* (New York: Dell Publishing Co., Inc., Delta Books, 1978), p. 24.

3. Ibid., p. 65.

4. Ibid., p. 180.

5. John Wu, *The Golden Age of Zen,* p. 47.

6. Ibid., p. 81.

7. Ibid., p. 78.

8. Ruth Sasaki, *The Record of Lin-chi* (Kyoto: The Institute for Zen Studies, 1975), p. 47.

9. For the relationship of the center to transference *see* Ernest Becker, *The Denial of Death,* p.129: "Freud saw that a patient in analysis developed a peculiarly intense attachment to the person of the analyst. The analyst became literally the center of his world and life."

10. Philip Yampolsky, *Zen Master Hakuin,* p. 118.

11. Ibid., p. 119.

12. Conway and Siegelman, *Snapping,* p. 24.

13. Anthony Mottola, tr., *The Spiritual Exercises of St. Ignatius* (New York: Doubleday & Co., Inc., Image Books, 1963), p. 139.

14. Igumen Chariton and P. Kadloubousky, tr., *The Art of Prayer* (Winchester, MA: Faber and Faber Inc., 1966), pp. 240–241.

15. Roselle Chartok and Jack Spencer, *The Holocaust Years* (New York: Bantam Books Inc., 1981), p. 127.

16. Ibid., p. 269.

17. Bea Pixa, *Taking Leave of the Ashram,* for "Sorting it Out," Berkeley, CA.

Chapter 9

1. Kapleau, *Mumonkan.*

2. Hakuin Zenji's "Chant in Praise of Zazen," *see* Kapleau, *Dawn in the West,* p. 183.

3. Miura and Sasaki, *Zen Dust,* pp. 68-69.

4. Chang Chung-yuan, *Original Teachings of Ch'an Buddhism,* p. 60.

5. Kapleau, *Mumonkan.*

6. Bunno Kato et al., tr., *The Threefold Lotus Sutra* (New York: John Weatherhill, Inc., 1975), p. 299.

7. Kapleau, *The Three Pillars of Zen,* p. 81

8. Kapleau, *Mumonkan.*

9. Kapleau, *Zen: Dawn in the West,* p. 183.

10. "Because meanings are dislocated—hidden in unexpected places, multiplied and split, given over to ambiguity, plurality, and uncertainty—the dream represents a decentered universe. . . . Such techniques of dream work as displacement, condensation, and distortion correspond to the tropes that create the dense, ambiguous polyvalent language of [*Finnegan's Wake*]. The tension in the language, which bars semantic certainty or simplicity, signifies the decentered universe it expresses." Margot Norris, *The Decentered World of Finnegan's Wake* (Baltimore, MD., John Hopkins University Press, 1976), pp. 7-8.

11. Quoted in Martin Heidegger, *Identity and Difference* (New York: Harper and Row Inc., Torch Books, 1960), p. 27.

12. O'Brien, *The Essential Plotinus,* p. 53.

13. Quoted by Harry Prock, *The Genesis of Philosophy* (New York: Doubleday & Co., Inc.), p. 294.

14. "Both [prajna and jnana] contain the root *jna* which signifies cognitive potentiality. . . ." If we look at the Tibetan translations for these terms we find the very same root connection has been preserved. The Tibetan for prajna is *shes-rab,* and for jnana is *ye-shes.* In both cases the *shes,* the cognitive potentiality, is there. *Ye* means "primordial" or "original." Thus ye-shes refers to primordial awareness. The Sanskrit prefix *pra* and the Tibetan particle *rab* have the sense of "heightening" or "intensification." To bring this (cognitive) potentiality to its highest pitch means to release it, to free it

from all the extraneous material that it has accumulated. Herbert V. Guenther and Chogyam Trungpa, *Dawn of Tantra* (Boulder, CO: Shambhala Publishing Inc., 1975), pp. 27–8.

15. Kapleau, *Zen: Dawn in the West,* p. 180.

16. D.T. Suzuki, tr., *Lankavatara Sutra* (Boulder, CO: Shambhala Publishing Inc., Prajna Press, 1978), p. xxi.

17. "Manas is the individual will to live and the principle of discrimination. . . . [it is] a double-headed monster, the one face looks towards the Alaya and the other looks towards the Vijnanas. . . . It is a double-edged sword. When there takes place a 'turning back' (paravritti) in it, the entire arrangement of things in the Vijnanakaya changes. . . . With one swing of the sword the pluralities are cut asunder. . . . The Alaya is absolutely One, but this oneness gains significance only when it is realized by Manas and recognized as its own supporter. . . ." After the 'turning back' "the external world is no more adhered to as such, that is, as reality; for it is no more than a mere reflection of the Alaya. The Alaya has been looking at itself in the Manas mirror." Suzuki, *The Lankavatara Sutra,* pp. xxiii–xxv. It is not suggested that there is a one-to-one relation between Manas and me-as-center/me-as-periphery, but that there is a remarkable parallel. *See also* the notion of *manas,* and *sparsa* in Herbert Guenther, "Mind and Its States" in *Philosophy and Psychology in the Abhidharma* (Boulder, CO: Shambhala Publishing Inc., 1976), pp. 4-36.

18. "We look at the world sideways. Instead of facing it as spectators we are in it and of it and we therefore see it partially and from a private perspective. Our view interprets and misinterprets our position in the world, a dilemma arising from the ambiguous function of the human mind. In a typically and perhaps exclusively human way we participate actively in our world, while at the same time trying to view it with the detachment of an observer." Arnheim, *The Power of the Center,* p. 16.

19. "In dealing with anorexia nervosa we are dealing with metaphor. It is for this reason, following on from Freud and Szasz, that I propose to treat my patient as a text. But I take my clue from the American critic Norman Holland. 'Unity is to the text as identity is to the person: or you could say, identity is the unity I find in a person when I look at him as if he were a text.' Given what has already been said about identity, it is unlikely that we shall find in the anorexic a unity of text. It is my belief

that anorexic speech (or, more literally, behavior) consists of two quite separate and often contradictory texts." Sheila McLeod, *The Art of Starvation* (New York: Doubleday & Co., Inc., Virago, 1982), p. 68.

20. Krishnamurti, *The Awakening of Intelligence*, p. 15.

21. Ibid., p. 25.

22. Ibid., p. 29.

23. Thich Thien-An, *Zen Philosophy: Zen Practice* (Berkeley, CA: Dharma Publishing, 1975), p. 152.

24. Chang Cheng-Chi, *The Practice of Zen* (London: Rider and Co., 1960), p. 78.

25. Rig Veda, 1164:20, quoted by Antonio T. de Nicolas, *Meditations through the Rig Veda* (New York: Nicholas Hays Ltd., 1976).

26. Kapleau, *Mumonkan*.

27. A.F. Price and Wong Mou-Lam, *The Diamond Sutra and The Sutra of Hui Neng* (Berkeley: The Clear Light Series, Shambhala, 1969).

28. This is a free adaptation of a verse quoted in Chang Chung-yuan, *Original Teachings of Ch'an Buddhism*, p. 176.

Chapter 10

1. Kapleau, *Mumonkan*.

2. Kapleau, *The Three Pillars of Zen*, p. 28

3. Ibid., p. 77.

4. T.S. Eliot, *Four Quartets*.

5. Ibid.

Chapter 11

1. Kapleau, *Hekiganroku*.

2. T.S. Eliot, *Four Quartets*.

3. Jack Henry Abbott, *In the Belly of the Beast* (New York: Random House Inc., Vintage Trade Books, 1982), p. 70.

4. G.R.S. Mead, *Hymn of Jesus* (London: John Watkins, 1963).

5. Sir Edwin Arnold, *Light of Asia* (New York: Doubleday Publishing Co., Dolphin Books, 1961), p. 86.

6. Quoted by R.D. Laing, *The Divided Self*, p. 78.

7. G.R.S. Mead, *Hymn of Jesus*.

8. Arthur Miller, *Death of a Salesman*.

9. Cyril Connolly, *The Unquiet Grave* (New York: Viking Press Inc., 1962), p. 46.

10. Primo Levi, *Survival in Auschwitz* (New York: Collier Books, 1961).

11. Wilfred Owen, "The Strange Meeting," *Collected Works of Wilfred Owen* (London: Chatto & Windus, 1963).

12. Sir Edwin Arnold, *Light of Asia*, p. 57.

13. Dante, Dorothy L. Sayers, tr., *Divine Comedy* (Harmondsworth, England: Penguin Books, 1950).

14. Russian fairy tale quoted by Thomas de Harmann, *Our Life with Mr. Gurdjieff* (Totowa, NJ: Cooper Square Publishing Inc., 1964), p. 3.

15. Dimock and Levertov, *In Praise of Krishna*, p. 21.

16. T.S. Eliot, *Four Quartets.*

17. St. John of the Cross, *The Dark Night of the Soul* (New York: Frederick Ungar Publishing Co., 1957), p. 40.

18. P.D. Ouspensky, *In Search of the Miraculous* (San Diego: Harcourt Brace Jovanovich Inc., 1949), p. 40.

19. Thomas Merton, *Wisdom of the Desert* (New York: New Directions Publishing Co., 1970), p. 61.

20. Ibid., p. 39.

21. Hubert Benoit, *The Supreme Doctrine* (London: Routledge & Kegan Paul, 1955,) p. 240.

22. Fritz Peters, *Boyhood with Gurdjieff* (London: Victor Gollancz Ltd., 1964), p. 96.

23. Merton, *Wisdom of the Desert*, p. 55.

24. R.H. Blyth, *Haiku.*

25. F.L. Woodward, *Some Sayings of the Buddha* (Oxford, England: Oxford University Press, 1973), pp. 14-15.

26. Carlos Castaneda, *Teachings of Don Juan: A Yaqui Way of Knowledge* (Berkeley: University of California Press, 1968).

27. Franz Kafka, *Letters to Milena.*

28. Heidegger, *Existence and Being*, p. 336.

29. Campbell, *The Hero with a Thousand Faces*, p. 60.

30. Robert A.F. Thurman, *The Holy Teaching of Vimalakirti* (University Park, PA: Pennsylvania State University Press, 1976), p. 43.

31. T.S. Eliot, *Four Quartets.*

Index

—A—

Adam, 131
Altar, as dynamic center, 115
Ambiguity, 14–15, 58, 100, 151;
    and the body, 179;
    as reality, 82;
    burden of, 83;
    defined, 58;
    fundamental, 15, 71, 87, 130, 162;
    of "me," 81;
    two faces of, 74
Anatman, 190
Anorexia nervosa, 236
Argentina, 113
Aristotle, 126, 137
Arjuna, 89
Arnheim, Rudolf, 67, 74–75
Atman, 190
Auschwitz, 208
Avalokitesvara, 172, 175
Awakened, 116
Awakening, 12, 93, 94, 163

—B—

Baso, 34, 114, 117
Becker, Ernest, 230, 234
Behaviorists, 79
Benoit, Huber, 118;
    quoted, 215
Bernstein, Leonard, 58
Bhagavad Gita, 89
Bhakti, 88
Big Bang, 136
Birdsong, 104
Bi-unity, 226
Black hole, 136
Bodhi, 171–72, 177
Bodhisattva, 172;
    of compassion, 219
Bohm, David, quoted, 82
Bonhoeffer, Dietrich, quoted, 41
Bo tree, 106, 190
Buber, Martin, 233
Buddha, 117, 147, 165–66;
    and Gnosticism, 54;
    and suffering, 24, 203–4;
    as Center, 116;
    as figure, 115;

as Gautama, 23;
as the Way, 166;
as unique one, 171;
defined, 12, 167;
quoted, 160
Buddhahood, 142
Buddha nature and Mu, 189
Buddha's teaching, 143–44
Buddhism, first noble truth
of, 121
Buddhist temple, 115
Bunuel, 53–54

—C—

Campbell, Joseph, 108
Center, 65–66, 74–76, 100,
105, 122–23, 126, 178,
182;
and periphery, 67–68;
and sacred tree, 105;
and territory, 103–4;
as ego, 107;
Buddha as, 106;
granting of, 78;
magic, 112;
needle as, 110–11;
of idea, 146;
sacrificed, 154
Christ, 85, 207;
and the Father, 82;
as Logos, 20;
quoted, 20, 25, 32, 147,
154, 161, 166;
relics of, 114
Christianity, 204
Christmas tree, 105
Concentration, 199–200
Conflict, 50, 69
Confucianism, 19
Conway, Flo, quoted, 148,
158

Crucifixion, 106
Cult, 148, 150, 160

—D—

Dante, quoted, 210
Devil, the, 125
Diamond Sutra, 14, 126,
141–43, 151, 176, 188
Dilemma, *see* Ambiguity
Dogen, 32–33, 39, 40, 123
Doubt, 31, 200
Duality, 204
Duhkha, 121, 204

—E—

Eckhart, 65, 70, 103
Ego, 15, 150, 162, 182
Egypt, 131
Eichmann, 55, 56
Einstein, Albert, 57
Eliade, Mircea, 106
Eliot, T.S., 101, 201, 202,
203, 212, 219
Enlightenment, 88–90
Est, 158
Eye, the, 73
Eyes, 76–77, 83, 86–87, 135

—F—

Faith, 31
Falklands, 113
Fear, 217–18
Flag, 116, 118
Form, 144
Freud, 41, 87

—G—

Galtieri, 113–14
Gandhi, 60
Gensha, 50
George, Leonard, 102–3

Gilgamesh, 21, 24
Gnostics, 54
God, 87, 88-89, 124, 129, 138, 213
Good, 204
Gordian knot, 74, 99, 227
Great death, 197
Gurdjieff, 97, 161, 215, 217
Gutei, 98, 143, 153, 166, 192

—H—

Haiku, 24
Hakuin, 33, 39, 156-57, 169, 173
Hegel, 175
Heidegger, 47, 127, 128, 218, 233
Heraclitus, 138
Hero with a Thousand Faces, 108
Hindu, 89
Hitler, 40, 41-42, 46-48, 97, 112-13, 192, 193
Holy Grail, 21
Hsu-yun, 107
Huang Po, 42
Hui-neng, 45, 150
Humiliation, 98, 157, 214-15
Hwa-yen, 222-23
Hyakujo, 29-31
Hymn of Jesus, 205

—I—

I, 97, 134
I am, 103, 145, 159
I am, 97, 103, 109, 110
I and it, 15, 110, 131-32, 135, 147, 148, 149
I and Thou, 82, 129

Idea, 146, 173
Irony, 13-14, 15, 221

—J—

Janus, 125
Jataka tales, 219
Jerusalem, 107
Jesus, 89
Jesus Christ Superstar, 85
Jnana, 88, 177, 235
Joshu, 17-18, 20-21, 161, 173, 182, 189, 190, 191
Jung, C.G., 102, 230

—K—

Kafka, 206
Kannon, 219
Kant, Immanuel, 175
Kapleau-roshi, 25, 30, 115-16, 162, 200
Keller, Helen, 123-24, 125
Knowing, 15, 171-72
Knowing/being, 172-74
Koan, 13-14, 16, 38, 151
Koans quoted:
　Hekigan Roku:
　　Echo asks about Buddha, 129;
　　Ejaku's "What is your name?", 81, 128;
　　Fuketsu's "One particle of dust," 194;
　　Layman P'ang's "Beautiful snowflakes," 117;
　　Tozan's "No cold or heat," 203
　Mumonkan:
　　Abandon words and silence, 125;

Mumonkan: (cont'd)
  A woman comes out
    of meditation, 165;
  Gutei raises a finger,
    36;
  Keichu's carts, 96,
    119;
  Mind is Buddha, 117;
  Mu, 189-90;
  No mind, no Buddha,
    117;
  Ordinary Mind is the
    Way, 14, 17;
  Ryutan blows out the
    candle, 141;
  Sei and her soul, 52;
  Shuzan and a staff, 63;
  Zuigan calls "master,"
    65
  Others:
  The iron cow, 9
Krishnamurti, 122, 182-83
Ku, 51

—L—
Laing, R.D., 72
Language, 125
Layman P'ang, 117, 188
Levi-Strauss, Claude, 227-28
Light, 89-91
Love, divine, 85-87;
  romantic, 84-86
Low, Albert, 91, 92, 94

—M—
Magic, 107, 125
Magic Center, *see* Center
Magic circle, 135
Mahakasyapa, 11
Mana, 104, 110;
  transference of, 114
Manas, 177, 236

Manjusri, 165, 166, 172,
  175, 176, 182, 195
Marx, 41
Mathematics, 136
Ma-Tsu, *see* Baso
Me, 73
Meaning, 119;
  as Logos, 20
Me-as-center/me-as-periph-
  ery, 72-73, 74, 76, 86,
  88, 177
Mecca, 106-7
Metaphor, 13
Milarepa, 160
Momyo, 179, 182, 186-87,
  188, 190
Montreal Zen Center, 22
Mu, 15, 94, 156, 199
Mu-chou, 152
Mumon, 117-18, 121, 122,
  124, 170
Mustard seed, 24, 206

—N—
Nagarjuna, 138
Nansen, 188, 204-5
Naropa, 160
Nazi, 48, 62, 80
Nazi Germany, 113
Nazism, 160
Nepal, 105
Nuremburg, 113

—O—
Obedience, 153-54
Observer, 178-79
Om, 199
One, the, 13, 36-45, 73-
  74, 82, 97-98;
  and two, 53, 55-57, 87,
  98-100;
  incarnation of, 107;

mind, 12, 145, 167;
the power of, 107
Oneness, 145;
and ambiguity, 15, 74;
and Buddha nature, 51;
and craving, 180–82;
and Id, 87;
and suffering, 99;
and training, 42–43;
as I am, 99;
as order, 49;
fundamental, 15;
not abstraction, 44;
yearning for, 149, 155
One-pointedness, 199
Other, 71–72, 76, 127
Ouspensky, P.D., 209

—P—

Pain, psychological, 98
Parmenides, 175
Plotinus, 31, 101, 175
Point, 100, 102, 145
Pope, the, 116
Po-shan, 185
Prajna, 176–77, 235
Prajna Parmita Hridya,
176
Psychoanalysis, 155
Psychotherapy, 146

—R—

Raja Yoga, 102
Ramana Maharishi, 98, 174
Religion, 41–42, 43, 119,
192
Renée, 75, 109, 111, 134–
35, 183
Rig Veda, 124
Rilke, Rainer, 101
Rinzai, 153
Russell, Bertrand, 136–37

—S—

Sacred relics, 114
Sacred tree, 105–6
Samadhi, 91–95, 174–75
Schizophrenia, 109
Sexuality, 104
Shakyamuni, *see* Buddha
Shankaracharya, 21
Shibayama, 42, 43
Siddhartha Gautama, *see*
Buddha
Siegelman, Jim, *see* Con-
way, Flo
Sin, 213
Singularity, 136
Six worlds, 98
Sleep, 174
Spengler, Oswald, 125
St. Francis, 192
St. Ignatius, 158
St. John, 124
St. John of the Cross, 85,
213
St. Thomas Aquinas, 137
Stupa, 114
Suffering, 16, 25, 121, 203–
10;
donkey suffering, 207
Sufi, 89, 102, 130
Sukha, 121
Sutra, Avatamsaka, 18;
Lankavatara, 18;
Surangama, 118, 147
Suzuki, 177

—T—

Tao, *see* the Way
Tathagata, 126
Teacher, 27, 29–31, 148,
152–58, 214–16
Teilhard de Chardin, 70, 74
Tenryu, 36–37

Term, 137
Territory, 103
Thatcher, Margaret, 113
Third Patriarch, 124, 148–
   49
Third Reich, 45
Tibetan Book of the Dead,
   95
Transference, 155
Tung-shan, 114

—U—
Ummon, 173
Uniqueness, 97–98, 154
Unus-ambo, 226–27
Uroborus, 77

—V—
Vesica Pisces, 225–26
Viewpoint, 70, 78, 107, 135

Vijnana, 177

—W—
Wave, 49
Way, 17, 18, 19, 154
Weil, Simone, 102
Whitehead, Alfred N., 41,
   48
Whitman, Walt, 125
Word, 15, 63, 122–30

—Y—
Yasutani-roshi, 29, 34, 43,
   51, 181
Yun-men, 114, 152–53

—Z—
Zazen, 32
Zendo, 115

NOTES

NOTES

A *koan* is a saying or action by a Zen master, probably the most famous being "What is the sound of one hand clapping?" Seemingly pointless or incomprehensible, a *koan* is actually an invitation to think in a new way, a tool to startle the consciousness into enlightenment. This remarkable series of essays, each beginning with an instructive *koan,* is a challenge to open the mind.

Drawing on the views of such diverse thinkers as Buddha, Bertrand Russell, Immanuel Kant, and T.S. Eliot to explain the essential concepts of Zen Buddhism, *The Iron Cow of Zen* is fascinating, thought-provoking reading. While all the chapters discuss humanity's basic ambiguity and the qualities required to break through to the truth of the world, each section focuses on a particular aspect of Zen Buddhism and can be read as a separate essay. Ultimately this montage of philosophical, historical, and literary references not only informs and entertains, but challenges the reader to view his existence in a different light.

Albert Low was born in England and holds a degree in philosophy and psychology. Since 1967 he has devoted full time to the practice of Zen Buddhism. He studied under Roshi Philip Kapleau and completed his training in 1986, at that time receiving full transmission as a teacher of Zen. Mr. Low is currently the director of the Montreal Zen Center, and the author of *An Invitation to Practice Zen* and *Zen and Creative Management.*

CHARLES E. TUTTLE COMPANY

90000

9 780804 816694

ISBN 0-8048-1669-7